# sommaire

## articles



## recensions d'ouvrages

# KNOWLEDGE, COMMUNICATION AND THE SCOTTISH ENLIGHTENMENT

SHEILA DOW*

**Résumé**
Cet article étudie les idées qu'Adam Smith et ses contemporains (en particulier Hume) ont développé sur la rhétorique en relation avec leur philosophie et leur analyse économique, tout en les situant dans le contexte des Lumières Écossaises. Les débats sur le langage en Écosse à cette époque se démarquaient des approches traditionnelles, lesquelles mettaient l'accent sur la persuasion ou le style, pour insister sur une notion plus large de communication intégrant ces deux préoccupations. Ceci découlait d'un intérêt pour les différences de langage. Pour Smith, cela découlait aussi de sa philosophie morale dans laquelle la communication est un moyen de persuasion en l'absence d'arguments démontrables. Le système de rhétorique qu'il a alors construit s'appuyait sur une distinction entre la construction d'un savoir (temporaire) par une méthode expérimentale et la communication de ce savoir ; communication dans laquelle la sympathie joue un rôle crucial. Une compréhension plus précise des vues de Smith sur la communication et le rôle de la sympathie auraient pu conduire à des interprétations différentes de son analyse économique, souvent mal comprise du fait d'une mauvaise interprétation de sa rhétorique.
**Mots-clés** : Adam Smith, rhétorique

* Professor in Economics, Director, SCEME, Department of Economics, University of Stirling, Stirling FK9 4LA, UK, Tel: +44 (0)1786-467474, Fax: +44 (0)1786-467469, s.c.dow@stir.ac.uk. This paper has benefited from the comments and suggestions of Deirdre McCloskey and two anonymous referees.

**Abstract**
There has been a recent resurgence of interest in the subject of rhetoric, including within economics. The purpose of the paper is to focus on the ideas on rhetoric of Adam Smith and his contemporaries (particularly Hume) in relation to their philosophy and economics, against the background of the Scottish Enlightenment. Discussions of language in Scotland at that time departed from what had become a conventional emphasis either on persuasion or on style in order to focus on a broader notion of communication which encompassed both. This followed from a focus on language differences within a united Britain. But for Smith it also followed from his moral philosophy, whereby communication was important as a vehicle for persuasion in the absence of scope for argument by demonstrable proof. He was thus concerned to set up a system of rhetoric. Smith distinguished between the derivation of (provisional) knowledge by the Newtonian experimental method, and the communication of that knowledge as if it were based on derivation from first principles. Subsequent (mis)interpretation of Smith's economics can be understood as stemming from mistaking the rhetoric for the method, and interpreting first principles as axioms. A fuller understanding of Smith's views on communication and the role of sympathy (through imagination) might have led to different understandings of Smith's economics prevailing.
**Keywords**: Adam Smith; rhetoric

**JEL codes**: B3, B4

## Introduction

The purpose of this paper is to consider the ideas about communication which evolved in Scotland in the eighteenth century, and which still have importance today with the revival of interest in the field. The study of rhetoric has a long history, going back to ancient Greece. In the pre-enlightenment period, rhetorical study had come to focus on literary criticism [1]. However, the eighteenth-century ideas on rhetoric in Britain reflected the growth

1. For example in Rapin's [1684] rhetorical study.

in natural science and the associated preference for a plainer style [2]. These ideas were developed in Scotland in a distinctive systematic way in being concerned, both with linguistic style from a literary perspective, and with metaphysics, or knowledge about the real world. The resulting synthetic approach to rhetoric was captured, not only in the content, but also in the title, of Adam Smith's [1762-63a] lectures on the subject: *Lectures on Rhetoric and Belles Lettres*. The aim here is to explore the system of rhetoric put forward by Smith, and to use Smith's own ideas on rhetoric in order to understand his economics and the way in which it has been interpreted. Because Smith was concerned with communication, both linguistic style and form of reasoning played a part in capturing the imagination of the audience.

We will discuss how, because the scientific method itself might differ from the most persuasive way of communicating ideas, the scope for misinterpretation was enhanced. Since scientific method and rhetoric differed for Smith himself, we can understand why Smith could be understood as the father of political economy (including its Austrian and Marxist forms) on the basis of his scientific method, and of general equilibrium theory on the basis of his rhetoric. We will consider these general interpretations of his economics in more detail below.

The broader Scottish enlightenment understanding of rhetoric as communication is something which has emerged in much of the modern literature on rhetoric. This is particularly the case in the context of economics, in the work of McCloskey [1985, 1994] [3]. McCloskey traces ideas on communication from classical times, and explores Smith's ideas on rhetoric as expressed in his *Lectures on Jurisprudence* [Smith 1762-63b], the *Theory of Moral Sentiments* [Smith 1759] and the *Wealth of Nations* [Smith 1776], rather than the *Lectures on Rhetoric* themselves, illustrating how embedded Smith's ideas on rhetoric were in his theory of knowledge and

2. This development arose from the work of Boyle [1663], Sprat [1667] and Locke [see Howell 1967].

3. See further http://deirdremccloskey.org/for references to her other extensive writing in this area.

indeed of human nature, more generally. Others have applied the theory of rhetoric to Smith's own writing. For example Warren Samuels has applied his rhetoric approach [Samuels 1989, Introduction] to an exploration of the different interpretations of Smith himself [Samuels 2009], while Vivienne Brown [1994] compares the rhetoric of the *Theory of Moral Sentiments* with that of the *Wealth of Nations.*

The approach to be taken here to presenting Smith's ideas will likewise emphasise the interconnections between different aspects of his *œuvre*, drawing on aspects of his context and apparent intentions, but drawing explicitly on the *Lectures on Rhetoric and Belles Lettres.* Indeed one of Smith's ideas on rhetoric was that, to understand a speaker or author, it is necessary to understand the spirit in which their ideas are being put forward. Here in this notion of an outside observer seeking to understand an author, with sympathy, we seem to have presentiment of the concept of the impartial spectator which he developed in the *Theory of Moral Sentiments* (something we will come back to below). Further, this historiographical approach, developed in modern times by Quentin Skinner [1969], facilitates our study of interconnections by seeing some continuity in an author's thought. But it puts a focus on the author which is challenged by another influential stream within modern rhetorical study. Particularly important for our consideration of Smith is Brown's [1994] thoughtful reading of Smith which emphasises understanding from the point of view of the reader rather than the author. However, as we proceed, we will discuss how Smith addresses issues of understanding among his audiences which allows discussion of different readings [4].

Smith's mentor and friend, David Hume, also emphasised the role of rhetoric. He refers to "contentment" with the outcome of enquiry, rather than "truth", and therefore his role in persuading his readers. "There is nothing which is not the subject of debate, and in which men of learning are not of contrary opinions. [...]

4. While Brown [1994, chap. 2] argues that Smith did not address issues of meaning (and thus the scope for different meanings) in his *Lectures on Rhetoric and Belles Lettres*, a study of his work as a whole provides a better understanding of these issues.

amidst all this bustle 'tis not reason, which carries the prize, but eloquence" [Hume 1739-40, xiv]. But it was Smith who developed his thoughts on rhetoric more fully, thoughts which were recorded in the form of notes taken of his lectures in Edinburgh, and later in Glasgow, in the form of the *Lectures on Rhetoric and Belles Lettres*.

The intellectual context for Smith and Hume was the enlightenment. This development occurred during a time of dramatic change in Scotland, as in the rest of Europe. Agricultural improvement and the beginnings of specialised factory production were increasing wealth and encouraging shifts of population into the cities. This experience raised questions for the newly-emerging social sciences – about how this new system would work economically, socially and morally [Young 1997]. To these were added the practical questions for what were called the natural sciences. The result was an intellectual ferment. This was compounded in Scotland by political change. The Union of Parliaments in 1707 had shifted the political centre to London, while the 1715 and 1745 Jacobite Rebellions had a profound effect on Scottish society. These were armed rebellions aimed at restoring the Stuart line to the British throne, with most (but not all) support from the Scottish Highlands, whose culture was then actively suppressed when the second rebellion failed. The Scottish Enlightenment thinkers were keen to make their contribution within a British context. Yet, on account of their experience within Scotland (and in Scotland within Britain), they were aware of issues of difference in culture and language in a way which their contemporaries elsewhere were not [Emerson 2008; Dow and Dow 2008].

Communication was central to all of this. New ideas were being developed, but had to be communicated successfully at a time when the relevant disciplines had not been fully established. The Scottish thinkers were acutely aware of communication problems at a variety of levels [Berry 1974; Howell 1975]. The Select Society in Edinburgh, of which Smith and Hume were members, took on the task of promoting southern English as the common language [Buchan 2003, pp. 128-130]. Smith and Hume's mentor, Frances Hutcheson, was the first in Scotland to lecture in English rather than Latin [Berry 1974]. English was not the first language of

Scotland. Most Scots in the Highlands and Islands had been Gaelic speakers, but that language was now banned after the Rebellions. Elsewhere in Scotland the first language was Scots, which could not be readily understood outside Scotland. Smith and Hume travelled widely on the Continent, and strove to speak in a form of English which could be better understood, both there and in England. It was an active matter for debate, how best to speak and write in English.

But it was not just a matter of successful translation from one language to another (the conduit metaphor of communication). Communication of ideas also involved persuasion with respect to particular understandings of reality. The enlightenment saw its key figures thinking about problems in a totally new way, and this had to be communicated persuasively if others were to follow. But in addition, in Scotland, there was an acceptance that true knowledge was unattainable. What was to be communicated, then, was not "truth", but a way of thinking about the world which made sense in terms of the listener's experience, and which provided solutions to pressing problems. The listener had to be persuaded to accept the speaker's judgment, even at the level of conceptualisation. Communication issues were therefore integral to the theory of knowledge.

In the next section we will explore further the theory of knowledge in the Scottish enlightenment, contrasting it with theories of knowledge elsewhere. We will see the relevance of the ideas on rhetoric which arose from this background when we apply them to Adam Smith himself in the interpretation of his economic writings. In particular, we will see the rhetorical force of the modern interpretation of him as a free-marketeer. This is not just a matter of antiquarian interest. The power of this interpretation has meant that many of Smith's ideas which do not fit into a general equilibrium framework, such as the importance of history, of social convention, of arts, of moral philosophy and indeed about methodology itself, have been lost to modern economics discourse[5]. We will see how different interpretations of Smith's use of rhetoric led to different interpretations of his economics. What Smith actually communicated, over the ages, was arguably not what he intended (but he would, at least in retrospect, have understood).

## Scottish moral philosophy

The enlightenment period in Europe is generally characterised as the Age of Reason. Rather than truth being the sole preserve of the Church – the product of revelation – science would establish truth by means of human reason. Influenced by René Descartes, the French enlightenment is most closely associated with the privileging of reason. The implication was that the real world could be explained by means of introspection and deductive logic. More important, reason could be used to justify actively changing the world; this period saw the rise of humanism. David Hume grappled with this approach, but eventually concluded that it was not an adequate basis for science. In particular, he concluded that reason could not prove existence, without which science could not begin. However, social convention, built up over centuries of experience, provided the basis for belief in existence. Here we have the beginnings of the Scottish theory of human nature, on which all other knowledge, according to Hume, should be built [see further Dow 2001]. What was being put forward was a form of logic which was neither purely inductive nor deductive, but which employed a pluralist approach to knowledge, as in Keynes's subsequent formulation of "human logic" [see Gerrard 1992][6].

Indeed a theory of human nature was needed to understand why we seek knowledge in the first place[7]. Hume and Smith both

5. This is the case, even allowing for the increased interest now in his *Theory of Moral Sentiments*; issues of interpretation arise here as with Smith's economics.

6. Keynes's philosophy was significantly influenced by Hume; see Carabelli [1988].

7. McCloskey [2006] explores the significance of moral sense in Scottish ethical theory, in contrast to Kant and Bentham's inability to explain the motivation behind ethics.

emphasised sentiment (including moral sentiment, or passion) as the starting point for actions beyond instinct, and for knowledge. Reason came later. They discussed the sense of awe and wonder we experience when we come across something new which we cannot explain [see Smith 1795]. This was the focus of Smith's (posthumously published) essay on the *History of Astronomy* [Smith 1795; see further Skinner 1976]. This sense of awe and wonder drives us to seek out explanations. The very idea of causal connection itself comes from our own experience; we become accustomed to one thing following another, such as pain whenever we hit our hand, which encourages the idea of cause itself, in that one might cause the other:

> It follows, then, that all reasonings concerning cause and effect, are founded on experience, and that all reasonings from experience are founded on the supposition, that the course of nature will continue uniformly the same. We conclude, that like causes, in like circumstances, will always produce like effects. [Hume 1739-40, p. 651]

But Hume and Smith argued that the real world is so complex, and the mechanisms so hidden, that we cannot hope to understand fully what these causal mechanisms are. We are driven psychologically, as we would say now, to seek explanations which accord as well as possible with our experience and conventional understandings. But it is in effect the human condition that we cannot reasonably expect to uncover truth.

Having been motivated to find an explanation, the preferred approach was the Newtonian experimental method, as this was understood in Scotland [see Comim 2006; Montes 2006][8]. Experiments as we now understand them were possible only in the physical sciences; in the social sciences it was history which provided the experimental evidence. Both Hume and Smith made detailed study of a wide range of historical episodes in a wide

8. Newton would provide another case study for different interpretations from different epistemological perspectives, in this case the perspectives of England and France, compared to Scotland.

variety of locations. From this study they derived provisional principles, which would then be confronted with some other example of experience to see if it fitted[9]. If so, the principle was confirmed. If not, the principle required modification. Modifications would be expected for application to different circumstances. This was very different from Descartes's logical deduction from axioms taken to be true, such as his famous "cogito ergo sum". One line of reasoning was derived from experience and was subject to modification in different contexts, while the other was derived from self-evident truths and had universal application. The philosophy of science was fundamentally different. Further, while Descartes relied only on introspection and reason, Smith emphasised other faculties too [see further Dow 2009].

A critical human faculty which assists the process of the formation of theories is the imagination. As Griswold [2006, p. 23] argues, "Smith presents the imagination as lying at the heart of both 'sympathy' and of intellectual endeavour". The imagination furnished the conjectures which filled in the gaps in the evidence, as well as the theoretical system in which those conjectures were formed. In communicating such theoretical systems, it was not surprising in such an age that Smith should talk about theories as being "imaginary machines". Theories appeal to our experience, but also to our imaginations, by providing simple explanations to ease our sense of wonder, and explanations which are aesthetically appealing [Comim 2006]. The invisible hand is an example of metaphor which allows us to understand Smith's notion of a system whereby the unintended consequences of individual actions may produce a beneficial outcome.

The imagination is also exercised through one of its products: sympathy [Smith 1759; see also Raphael 1985]. While sympathy is fundamental to social behaviour in Scottish enlightenment thought (and indeed to the notion of identity [see Davis 2003]), it is also important for the mutual relations between author and reader, between speaker and audience. Successful communication requires

9. Because (inevitably) partial evidence leaves gaps to be filled by conjectures, this approach is sometimes referred to as conjectural history.

that the writer or speaker attempts to see the matter from the perspective of the reader or audience. As Robert Burns [1786] put it: "O wad some Power the giftie gie us, To see oursels as ithers see us!" [10]. How to communicate ideas in a persuasive manner is the subject of rhetoric, where imagination plays a central role. Let us turn now to focus on Smith's ideas on rhetoric.

## SMITH'S RHETORIC

Adam Smith's first employment, following attendance at Glasgow University and then Oxford University (where he no doubt improved his command of English), was to offer a series of private lectures in rhetoric in Edinburgh in 1748-1749 which, unusually for that time, were delivered in English. Smith was to continue to give these lectures when he took up the Chair in Logic and Rhetoric, and again as Professor of Moral Philosophy, in Glasgow. The *London Times* [1790] obituary referred to Smith's "pronunciation and style", which were "much superior to what could, at that time, be acquired in Scotland only". At a time when Scottish thinkers were anxious to play on a wider stage, a discussion of language and presentation by someone recognised for his language skills attracted a ready audience.

Indeed much of Smith's lectures concerned linguistic style and how best to communicate clearly [Skinner 1996; Howell 1975]. For example, he argued for a plain style, avoiding elaborate figures of speech. While the plain style would reduce the scope for stirring the imagination and thus sympathy by style itself, it opened up scope for engaging sympathy through such devices as metaphors and references to telling episodes (such as the pin factory example with which he opens the *Wealth of Nations*) [11]; Smith also argued against a scholastic style, recounting all aspects of a subject.

10. In translation (by the present author) from Scots: "O would that some Power would give us the gift of seeing ourselves as others see us".

11. It is Smith's emphasis on the value of the plain style which Brown [1994] argues suppresses issues of meaning, while he in fact employs figures of speech himself in the *Lectures on Rhetoric and Belles Lettres*.

Further, when trying to convey others ideas, Smith regarded it as important to try to bring alive the spirit of the author. This enlivens our imaginations such that a sympathetic bond is built up between author and reader, between speaker and audience, which aids communication. Thus James Boswell [1785], the diarist, gives us an example based on his attendance at Smith's lectures on rhetoric. He remembered the pleasure Smith said he felt, when reading Milton, in knowing that the author laced his shoes with latchets, rather than buckled them. So this story clearly appealed to Boswell's imagination too.

Smith paid attention to the experience of the audience and what would appeal to their imagination. This in turn required the author to use imagination to understand the reader's perspective. The main focus of rhetoric had previously been either on oratory (designed to instruct and persuade), or on style and use of figures of speech. But Smith extended the subject to include, not only oratory, but also historical, or narrative, discourse, as well as poetic discourse [see Howell 1975]. This followed directly from the need to justify theories in relation to experience, so communicating theories also in relation to narration of experience. Persuasive discourse was thus an important part, but not the whole, of Smith's communicative discourse.

We can see an illustration of the idea of invoking the sympathy of the audience in Hume's *Treatise* [1739-40], where he aims to take rationalist argument as far as he can (but concludes with skepticism). Near the end of the first Book he states that, after grappling with metaphysical problems by means of pure reason:

> I am confounded with all these questions, and begin to fancy myself in the most deplorable condition imaginable, invironed with the deepest darkness, and utterly deprived of the use of every member and faculty.
>
> Most fortunately it happens, that since reason is incapable of dispelling these clouds, nature herself suffices to that purpose, and cures me of this philosophical melancholy and delirium, either by relaxing this bent of mind, or by some avocation, and lively impression of my senses, which obliterate all these chimeras. I dine, I play a game of backgammon, I converse, and am merry

> with my friends; and when after three or four hours' amusement, I would return to these speculations, they appear so cold, and strained, and ridiculous, that I cannot find in my heart to enter into them any farther.
> Here then I find myself absolutely and necessarily determined to live, and talk, and act like other people in the common affairs of life. [Hume 1739-40, p. 269]

This conjures up a lovely picture of the person the French referred to as "le bon David", out for an evening's entertainment in Edinburgh's Old Town with his friends [see further Graham's 2004, biography]. But it is also persuasive in fostering the view he came to about the need to ground metaphysics in real experience which, as we have seen, was to prove important for the development of ideas about economics and about rhetoric.

Smith approached rhetoric as he approached all subjects, attempting to identify a system – something which he clearly found appealed to his own imagination [Skinner 1996]. His system of rhetoric was integral to his philosophy more generally [Berry 1974]. As Bryce puts it in his Introduction to the *Lectures on Rhetoric and Belles Lettres* [Smith 1762-3, p. 25], "The primacy he gives to language [...] rests on his vision of language as the embodiment of the mind's striving towards the 'metaphysical', towards conceptualization". One of the students in Smith's logic class in Glasgow, John Miller, put his impressions of the lectures on rhetoric as follows: "the best method of explaining and illustrating the various powers of the human mind, the most useful part of metaphysics, arises from an examination of the several ways of communicating our thoughts by speech, and from an attention to the principles of those literary compositions, which contribute to persuasion and entertainment..." [*Royal Society of Edinburgh* 1794, pp. 616-612]. In rhetoric, as in other areas, Smith was able to put together new ideas, which were being formulated more widely in Scotland in such a new and systematic way that his rhetoric was highly persuasive. As Tribe [1999, p. 618] puts it, "he treated the domain of rhetoric as equivalent to human communication, and therefore a pathway to an understanding of human motivation".

While theories, in the Scottish approach to science, were derived from detailed study of experience, the communication of theories did not need to follow the same sequence. Indeed Smith argued that presenting theories as being derived from first principles was more persuasive than treating each experience in isolation – even if that is not how theories are arrived at [Skinner 1996]. Smith thus understood well why Descartes' ideas had been so persuasive. Nevertheless, being unpersuaded himself by Descartes' rationalism, Smith regarded Descartes' physics as "one of the most entertaining romances that have ever been wrote" [Smith 1762-63a, p. 146]. This distinction between how ideas are arrived at and how they are communicated will prove to be important for how Smith himself came to be understood.

## Rhetoric and economic theory

We can see an example of this disparity between the formation of ideas and their communication in Smith's [1776] most famous work, *An Inquiry into the Nature and Causes of the Wealth of Nations.* One of the principles which Smith had derived from his detailed historical study was the principle of the division of labour. Wealth is created as a result of specialisation; this was one of the main reasons for arguing for free trade – that it allowed for more specialisation and thus higher productivity. But, instead of arriving at this conclusion late in the work, Smith started the first chapter with the division of labour, as if it were one of Descartes's axioms. He explained it in terms of an example which some regard as apocryphal: the pin factory. This example appeals to our imaginations – we can imagine how difficult it would be for each of us to make our own pins, compared to a factory, where production is broken down into specialist steps. Further examples are given which reinforce our acceptance of the principle. Then the implications of the principle of the division of labour are drawn out.

I have just referred to Adam Smith's own communications. But communication of ideas was itself seen by Smith and Hume as integral to economic development [Dow and Dow 2008] [12]. Trade itself requires successful communication between buyer and seller – there must be some capacity to understand the other's point of view in order to engage in successful trade, even while pursuing self-interest. Further, trade exposes importers to new ideas about consumption, which sparks off ideas about possibilities for local production; thus other countries catch up with the first developers. Also the division of labour is enhanced by new ideas about developing production techniques which arise from communication. Workers learn new practices and forms of self-discipline in the workplace through communication [Wennerlind 2006].

Hume and Smith also studied how communication goes through its own process of development as an integral element of social and economic development – the organic view of language [Berry 1974]. This compounds the difficulty in understanding older texts. Smith speaks across the centuries, but is not necessarily understood in the same way. Indeed the interpretations of Smith are legion, differing at a range of levels, as Samuels [2009] explains with respect to the invisible hand. In the next section we draw on our understanding of Smith's rhetorical theory to help us understand the different interpretations of Smith, focusing on the invisible hand, the impartial spectator and the theory of economic development.

## Modern interpretation of Smith

Smith is most commonly associated with the concept of the invisible hand, a metaphor, which appeals to the imagination, for the apparently spontaneous successful workings of free market economies made up of selfish individuals [Tribe 1999]. But we only have to reflect on the well-known influence of Smith on Marx (a connection emphasised by Heilbroner [1986]) to appreciate the scope for different readings of Smith, such that we cannot

12. See McCloskey [1994, pp. 77-83]; McCloskey and Klamer [1995] and McCloskey [2006, pp. 306-307] for more general statements of this argument.

reasonably classify him as an out-and-out free marketeer. Indeed the conventional understanding in the modern history of economic thought literature is that the expression above of the invisible hand concept is misleading [see e.g. Winch 1997]. As Evensky [2005, chap. 10] puts it, we can differentiate between the "Chicago Smith" and the "Kirkcaldy Smith". On the one hand, self-interest is now understood to be conditioned by moral sentiments rather than being equivalent to selfishness, and on the other hand Smith noted the tendency for free competition to be limited. Indeed the one use of the term "invisible hand" in the *Wealth of Nations* [Smith 1776, IV.ii. 9] refers to the unintended consequences of bias in favour of domestic over foreign direct investment. This is intended as an indication of the scope for different interpretations: Samuels demonstrates the many and subtle differences in which the invisible hand has been interpreted.

Nevertheless the general equilibrium interpretation became embodied in much of modern economics, deduced from axioms of selfish rational individual behaviour [see e.g. Arrow and Hahn 1971]. So, arguably, what has happened is that Smith's rhetoric was mistaken for his scientific method. Smith arrived at his (provisional) principles based on detailed study of societies, but presented them as if on the basis of established principles which could be treated as axioms. Indeed Smith [1762-63a, p. 146] noted how appealing argument from first principles could be, being more persuasive than the Aristotelian style. But the distinction between (provisional) principles and axioms had not been successfully conveyed. So Smith would in fact have understood why his system was interpreted as Cartesian, even if that conflicted with everything else he wrote – about scientific method and about human nature. This also meant that his economic theory has been open to the interpretation, from a Cartesian perspective, of being the forerunner of general equilibrium theory [see Montes 2006].

However Smith's system of rhetoric was after all intended as a contribution to metaphysics, since communication and persuasion were essential aspects of the production of knowledge which rests on social convention, including conventional belief. Because truth was inaccessible, the notion of true axioms was ruled out. So, rather than presenting free-market principles as universals, in fact he pointed out ways in which market functions might be eroded – by producers trying to limit competition [Smith 1776, p. 84, p. 267], or by workers' lives being blighted by repetitive tasks [p. 782], for example. His conclusions for economic theory and policy were provisional, and open to the need for change in different circumstances. Smith was forceful in his rhetoric – he was keen to persuade; but this is perfectly compatible with an acceptance that Smith was offering theories which were not "true", and certainly not universally true, even if he thought they were the most persuasive according to his own imagination and experience.

Smith's notion of the impartial spectator provides another example of a concept which has been the subject of a range of interpretations. For Smith, knowledge was founded on sentiment and imagination, as well as experience. A major motivation in the eighteenth century for analysing the emerging specialised market economies was the concern that they would erode moral values (see e.g. Hont and Ignatieff (eds.) [1983] on the Scottish enlightenment, and Young [1997] specifically on Smith). In *The Theory of Moral Sentiments*, Smith [1759] explored the intrinsically social aspect of human nature, where sympathy plays a crucial role. It is sympathy with an imagined impartial spectator, as much as with the opinion of our neighbours, which keeps us in moral check [Raphael 1985; Griswold 2006]. It is now generally agreed among Smith scholars that the self-interested individual of the *Wealth of Nations* is consistent with the social being of the *Moral Sentiments*, bound by moral constraints embodied in the imagined judgement of the impartial spectator [Winch 1997; McCloskey 2008].

This understanding of Smith comes from taking seriously his system of rhetoric, and applying it to his own work. What we have now was published posthumously, based on students' notes which only emerged in 1961. Had Smith had more confidence in his own thoughts on rhetoric, and his lectures published earlier, then perhaps his own use of rhetoric, and its connection with his moral philosophy, would have led to a different interpretation of his economics. However it is only recently that economists beyond the history of economic thought have extended their attention to *The*

*Theory of Moral Sentiments*, and this has tended to be constrained by considering it in terms of a framework which is closer to Cartesian than Smithian. Thus for example Ashraf *et alii* [2005] interpret the impartial spectator, not as a source of moral restraint, but as the vehicle for rationality to prevail over sentiment in the long run. Alternatively Binmore [2005, p. 50] provides another interpretation of the impartial spectator as the exogenous imposer of some absolute concept of the Good. But Smith had emphasised in his theory of rhetoric the importance of imagination and (moral) sentiment, conditioned by the social nature of our understanding (alongside reason), for the successful communication of ideas. Moral judgement is neither reason overcoming sentiment, nor externally imposed, but rather the result of "judgement being shaped by the views of others" [Broadie 2006, p. 158]. This applies to internal communication with an imagined moral arbiter as much as to external communication of a speaker with his audience.

We might also have had for longer a better understanding of the Scottish enlightenment thought on progress, and comparisons between different societies. Scottish thought on economic development is often portrayed as a matter of inevitable progress from one stage to another. But, when the Scottish thinkers discussed the sequence of stages of social and economic development, it was clear that they did not see it in that way. They referred to other societies at earlier stages of economic development, with respect, and in fact addressed the problem that moral values might be eroded in later stages of development [Meek 1976]. This reflected not only the Scottish theory of knowledge, but also their sense of "otherness" with respect to other societies in spite of the commonalities in human nature. This sense of "otherness" arguably underpinned their epistemology (particularly the inaccessibility of absolute truth) and their methodology (particularly a focus on the provisionality of principles) [13]. Adam Ferguson [1767], the father of modern sociology, was particularly concerned that the socio-economic system would self-destruct as the social fabric was

13. The importance more generally of the sense of otherness has been most fully developed by Kaul [2008, chap. 2 and 3].

eroded by increasing commercialisation. He was a Highlander and Gaelic speaker who would have been aware even more than his Lowland friends of the dangers of making judgements about different social systems as indicating savagery.

## CONCLUSION

If nothing else, the theory of knowledge in the Scottish Enlightenment allowed for different approaches to, and versions of, knowledge. Social convention and moral values were critical to the successful functioning of society; reason alone was inadequate as a basis for improvement. This provided the basis for respect for difference. The system of rhetoric provided grounding for successful communication in spite of difference. The connection made between communication and understanding could still stand us in good stead in modern economics.

## REFERENCES

ARROW K.J. and HAHN F.H., 1971, *General Competitive Analysis*, San Francisco-Edinburgh, Holden Day-Oliver & Boyd.

ASHRAF N., CAMERERER C.F. and LOEWENSTEIN G., 2005, "Adam Smith, Behavioural Economist", *Journal of Economic Literature*, 19(3), pp. 131-145.

BERRY C., 1974, "Adam Smith's Considerations on Language", *Journal of the History of Ideas*, 35(1), pp. 130-138.

BINMORE K., 2005, *Natural Justice*, Oxford, Oxford UP.

BOSWELL J., 1925 (1785), *The Journal of a Tour to the Hebrides with Samuel Johnson, LL.D.*, London, T. Nelson.

BOYLE R., 1965 (1663), *Some considerations Touching the Style of the Holy Scriptures*, *in* T. Birch (ed.), *The Works of the Honourable Robert Boyle*, vol. 2, Hildersheim, Georg Olms.

BROADIE A., 2006, "Sympathy and the Impartial Spectator", *in* K. Haakonssen (ed.), *The Cambridge Companion to Adam Smith*, Cambridge, Cambridge UP.

BROWN V., 1994, *Adam Smith's Discourse: Canonicity, Commerce and Conscience*, London, Routledge.

BUCHAN J., 2003, *Capital of the Mind: How Edinburgh Changed the World*, Edinburgh, John Murray.

BURNS R., 1990 (1786), "Tae a Louse", in *The Complete Illustrated Poems, Songs and Ballads*, London, Chancellor, pp. 141-142.

CARABELLI A., 1988, *On Keynes's Method*, London, Macmillan.

COMIM F., 2006, "Scottish Common Sense Philosophy", *in* A. Dow and S. Dow (eds.), *A History of Scottish Economic Thought*, London, Routledge, pp. 123-145.

DOW A. and DOW S., 2008, "Theories of Economic Development in the Scottish Enlightenment", *in* P.E. Earl and B. Littleboy (eds.), *Regarding the Past*, Brisbane, University of Queensland, pp. 9-24.

DOW S., 2001, "Hume: A Re-assessment", *in* P.L. Porta, R. Scazzieri and A.S. Skinner (eds.), *Knowledge, Division of Labour and Social Institutions*, Cheltenham, Edward Elgar, pp. 75-92.

–, 2009, "Smith's Philosophy and Economic Methodology", *in* J.T. Young (ed.), *Elgar Companion to Adam Smith*, Cheltenham, Edward Elgar.

EMERSON R.L., 2008, "The Scottish Contexts for David Hume's Political-Economic Thinking", *in* C. Wennerlind and M. Schabas (eds.), *David Hume's Political Economy*, London, Routledge.

EVENSKY J., 2005, *Adam Smith's Moral Philosophy*, Canbridge, Cambridge UP.

FERGUSON A., 1967 (1767), *Essay on the History of Civil Society*, D. Forbes (ed.), Edinburgh, Edinburgh UP.

GERRARD B., 1992, "Human Logic in Keynes's thought: Escape from the Cartesian Vice", *in* P. Arestis and V. Chick (eds.), *Recent Developments in Post-Keynesian Economics*, Cheltenham, Edward Elgar.

GRAHAM R., 2004, *The Great Infidel: A Life of David Hume*, Edinburgh, Tuckwell.

GRISWOLD C.L. Jr., 2006, "Imagination: Morals, Science, and Arts", *in* K. Haakonssen (ed.), *The Cambridge Companion to Adam Smith*, Cambridge, Cambridge UP.

HEILBRONER R.L., 1986, *The Essential Adam Smith*, Oxford, Oxford UP.

HONT I. and IGNATIEFF M. (eds.), 1983, *Wealth and Virtue: The Shaping of Political Economy in the Scottish Enlightenment*, Cambridge, Cambridge UP.

HOWELL W.S., 1967, "John Locke and the New Rhetoric", *Quarterly Journal of Speech*, 53, pp. 319-333.

–, 1975, "Adam Smith's Lectures on Rhetoric: An Historical Assessment", *in* A.S. Skinner and T. Wilson (eds.), *Essays on Adam Smith*, Oxford, Clarendon, pp. 11-43.

HUME D., 1978 (1739-40), *A Treatise of Human Nature*, K.A. Selby-Bigge and P.H. Nedditch (eds.), 2 e ed., Oxford, Clarendon.

KAUL N., 2008, *Imagining Economics Otherwise: Encounters with Identity/Difference*, London, Routledge.

*London Times*, 1790, "Obituary of Adam Smith", 24 July.

MCCLOSKEY D.N., 1994, *Knowledge and Persuasion in Economics*, Cambridge, Cambridge UP.

–, 2006, *The Bourgeois Virtues: Ethics for an Age of Commerce*, Chicago, Chicago UP.

–, 2008, "Adam Smith, the Last of the Virtue Ethicists", *History of Political Economy*, 40(1), pp. 43-71.

— and KLAMER A., 1995, "One Quarte of GDP is Persuasion", *American Economic Review*, 85(2), pp. 191-195.

MEEK R.L., 1976, *Social Science and the Ignoble Savage*, Cambridge, Cambridge UP.

MONTES L., 2006, "Adam Smith: Real Newtonian", *in* A. Dow and S. Dow (eds.), *A History of Scottish Economic Thought*, London, Routledge, pp. 102-122.

RAPHAEL D.D., 1985, *Adam Smith*, Oxford, Oxford UP.

RAPIN R., 2009 (1684/1706), *The Whole Critical Works of Monsieur Rapin*, Whitefish (MT), Kessinger.

*Royal Society of Edinburgh*, 1794, *Transactions*, vol. III, pt. I.

SAMUELS W.J. (ed.), 1989, *Economics as Discourse: An Analysis of the Language of Economics*, Boston, Kluwer.

–, 2009, "The Invisible Hand", *in* J.T. Young (ed.), *Elgar Companion to Adam Smith*, Cheltenham, Edward Elgar.

SKINNER A.S., 1976, "Adam Smith: The Development of a System", *Scottish Journal of Political Economy*, 23(2), pp. 111-132.

–, 1996, "Language, Rhetoric and the Communication of Ideas", in *A System of Social Science: Papers Related to Adam Smith*, 2 e ed., Oxford, Clarendon, pp. 7-24.

SKINNER Q., 1969, "Meaning and Understanding in the History of Ideas", *History and Theory*, 8, pp. 3-53.

SMITH A., 1976 (1759), *The Theory of Moral Sentiments* (Glasgow edition), D.D. Raphael and A. Macfie (eds.), Oxford, Oxford UP.

–, 1983 (1762-63a), *Lectures on Rhetoric and Belles Lettres*, J.C. Bryce (ed.), Oxford, Oxford UP.

–, 1978 (1762-63b), *Lectures on Jurisprudence* (A), R.L. Meek, D.D. Raphael and P.G. Stein (eds.), Oxford, Oxford UP.

–, 1976 (1776), *An Inquiry into the Nature and Causes of the Wealth of Nations*, R.H. Campbell and A.S. Skinner (eds.), Oxford, Oxford UP.

–, 1980 (1795), "The History of Astronomy", in *Essays on Philosophical Subjects*, W.L.D. Wightman (ed.), Oxford, Oxford UP.

SPRAT T., 1667, *The History of the Royal Society of London*, London.

TRIBE K., 1999, "Adam Smith: Critical Theorist?", *Journal of Economic Literature*, 37(2), pp. 609-632.

WENNERLIND C., 2006, "David Hume as a *Political* Economist", *in* A. Dow and S. Dow (eds.), *A History of Scottish Economic Thought*, London, Routledge, pp. 46-70.

WINCH D., 1997, "Adam Smith's Problem and Ours", *Scottish Journal of Political Economy*, 44(4), pp. 384-402.

YOUNG J.T., 1997, *Economics as a Moral Science: The Political Economy of Adam Smith*, Cheltenham, Edward Elgar.

# RÉCONCILIER LE FORMEL ET LE CAUSAL : LE RÔLE DE LA NEUROÉCONOMIE

BENOIT HARDY-VALLEE ET BENOÎT DUBREUIL*

**Résumé**

La théorie du choix rationnel (TCR), dans son interprétation standard, ne se présente pas comme une théorie causale, mais bien normative. L'économie expérimentale, en remplaçant les hypothèses sous-jacentes à l'interprétation standard de la TCR par des hypothèses plus réalistes – une fonction d'utilité qui inclut des préférences sociales, par exemple – a permis d'améliorer la prédictivité de la TCR. En revanche, elle n'est pas parvenu à surmonter une autre difficulté théorique à laquelle fait face la TCR, à savoir l'absence d'ancrage causal des entités formelles postulées. Dans cet article, nous montrons comment la neuroéconomie, parce que son étude ne se limite pas à des manifestations comportementales, *laisse* entrevoir le développement d'une véritable science naturelle de la décision.

**Mots-clés** : théorie du choix rationel, neuroéconomie, économie expérimentale, jeu de l'ultimatum

* Remerciements : la recherche de Benoit Hardy-Vallée a été rendue possible par une bourse postdoctorale du Conseil de recherche en sciences humaines du Canada et celle de Benoît Dubreuil par un mandat d'aspirant du Fonds de la recherche scientifique et une bourse postdoctorale du Fonds québécois de recherche sur la société et la culture. Nous remercions un évaluateur anonyme pour ses commentaires généreux sur une version précédente de cet article.

Benoit Hardy-Vallee : Decision Support Services, SBR Global, Toronto, benoit@hardyvallee.net.

Benoît Dubreuil : Département de philosophie, Université du Québec à Montréal, Case postale 8888, succursale Centre-ville, Montréal, Québec, Canada, H3C 3P8, dubreuil.benoit@uqam.ca.

**Abstract**
Rational choice theory (RCT) is standardly interpreted not as a causal theory, but as a normative one. Experimental economics, by replacing underlying assumptions of the standard interpretation of RCT by more realistic ones – by including pro-social preferences to the utility function, for instance – has improved the predictability of the RCT. That was not sufficient, however, to overcome another theoretical difficulty that RCT faces, which is the fact that its postulated entities are not rooted in any causal mechanism. In this paper, we show how neuroeconomics, because it is not limited to behavioral manifestations, may pave the way to the development of a natural science of decision-making.
**Keywords**: Rational choice theory, neuroeconomics, experimental economics, ultimatum game

**Classification JEL** : A12, B13, C79, D01, D87

## Introduction

De Pappus d'Alexandrie à Crick et Watson, la mise au jour de mécanismes a contribué à l'explication de la nature. Par *mécanisme*, on entend une analyse du fonctionnement d'un système qui décompose celui-ci en éléments, chacun pouvant effectuer certaines opérations, puis qui montre comment les caractéristiques du système résultent de l'activité des éléments. On peut distinguer deux interprétations du mécanisme, l'une causale, l'autre formelle. Dans le premier cas, les éléments du mécanisme ont des contreparties matérielles : pour chaque élément de l'explication ou du modèle, on peut identifier une structure réelle, matérielle, capable d'interaction causale. (Notons que par causalité, nous entendons ici une notion réaliste telle que le transfert d'énergie.) Le diagramme d'un moteur à explosion, par exemple, représente des pièces (piston, bielle, soupape) qui peuvent être identifiées dans un moteur réel.

Dans le second cas, le mécanisme décrit des éléments et des opérations sans pour autant que ceux-ci ne soient appariés à des structures matérielles : on vise plutôt l'adéquation entre les relations fonctionnelles (entrés/sorties) du modèle et celles du système à l'étude. Ainsi la linguistique chomskyenne propose un modèle mécaniste-formel d'explication de la compétence linguistique en supposant des éléments (par exemple, les groupes nominaux ou verbaux) ainsi que des opérations (les règles de formation et de transformation des phrases). Les éléments comme les opérations, cependant, ne correspondent pas à des structures neuronales, anatomiques ou moléculaires, mais à un ensemble de processus computationnels. Les modèles chomskyens rendent compte de la compétence linguistique humaine, mais n'expliquent pas, par exemple, comment nos aires motrices et auditives interagissent afin de produire et comprendre des phrases.

La théorie économique a, en général, opté pour une approche formelle de la rationalité, en particulier depuis l'adoption de la conception *ordinale* de l'utilité. Auparavant, dans la psychologie hédoniste de Bentham et de Mill, l'utilité était un étalon de mesure du bonheur global de l'individu, qui subsumait en une dimension les variétés de plaisirs et de douleurs. On représentait alors l'utilité comme une valeur objective et en principe mesurable, une utilité *cardinale*. Elle comportait toutefois une incertitude relative à sa mesure, et c'est pourquoi le premier pas vers la formalisation du choix rationnel fut l'abandon de la conception cardinale de l'utilité pour une logique des préférences comparées.

Dans la théorie de l'utilité *ordinale*, la décision économique peut être construite sans hypothèses psychologiques sur l'intensité ou le contenu des sensations ou perceptions. En effet, plutôt que d'ordonner les choix de l'agent en fonction de leur propension objective à maximiser son bien-être, la théorie s'intéresse plutôt à l'ordonnancement des préférences de l'agent. L'utilité devient ainsi une notion relationnelle plutôt qu'absolue, qui définit une relation de préférence entre deux alternatives : « A est préféré à B » équivaut à « A est plus utile que B ». Un agent économique n'a pas à être capable d'attribuer une valeur absolue à un choix A, mais doit simplement déterminer si 1) A est préférable à B, 2) B est préférable à A ou 3) A et B sont équivalents. De la sorte, utilité et préférences deviennent deux notions indissociables, l'utilité référant à l'échelle sur laquelle se mesurent les préférences relatives et subjectives, et les préférences définissant une fonction d'utilité.

## 1. Le formalisme à l'épreuve de l'expérience

La préférence est donc la notion première de la rationalité économique : la théorie de la décision, la théorie des jeux et la théorie de l'équilibre général modélisent l'agent rationnel comme celui qui sélectionne des décisions ou stratégies optimales, soit les possibilités d'action – parmi celles qui lui sont offertes – qui maximisent son utilité subjective. L'explication et la prédiction du comportement rationnel s'effectuent donc en identifiant des éléments – des états, des actions et des issues, selon le modèle de Leonard Savage [1954] – et leurs relations. La prise de décision est alors représentée par une mécanique formelle et la valeur du modèle se mesure à sa capacité à décrire le comportement du système à l'étude, plutôt qu'à le décomposer en entité causalement interactives. Avec les axiomatisations de von Neumann-Morgenstern, Savage et Arrow-Debreu, la science économique réalise l'idéal de « newtonisation » des sciences humaines.

Les préférences, stratégies et fonctions d'utilité fournissent une explication mécaniste de la prise de décision mais sans s'engager sur le plan ontologique. Aussi la théorie du choix rationnel (TCR), en elle-même, n'est-elle qu'un formalisme mathématique et non une théorie comportementale ou psychologique. Comme le résume Binmore [1994, p. 150], la pratique standard en économie est de considérer les théories de la rationalité comme des exercices formels :

> Des axiomes sont proposés et les propriétés des individus rationnels en sont alors déduites mathématiquement. Si les mathématiques nécessaires sont suffisamment évidentes, l'attention se concentre alors sur la vérité des théorèmes de l'auteur plutôt que [...] sur leur aptitude à formaliser les concepts qu'ils prétendent capturer.

On doit donc adjoindre à la TCR des hypothèses auxiliaires afin d'en faire un discours qui puisse être utilisé dans l'analyse empirique – sans pour autant en faire une mécanique *causale*. L'interprétation standard de la TCR s'est appuyée sur deux hypothèses : 1) le postulat de rationalité et 2) l'attribution d'une fonction d'utilité égoïste. Selon la première, on tient pour acquis que les agents sont rationnels, au sens où l'on présuppose une cohérence entre leurs croyances, désirs et intentions : par exemple l'intention de faire *A* doit pouvoir, du moins en théorie, être déduite des croyances et désirs de l'agent à propos de *A*. Selon la seconde, les individus possèdent une fonction d'utilité qui les amène à préférer leur intérêt individuel, défini généralement en termes monétaires.

L'ajout de ces hypothèses auxiliaires permet à la TCR de quitter le simple formalisme mathématique et de réaliser des prédictions empiriques. On peut désormais déduire les préférences d'un agent de sa fonction d'utilité et déterminer l'action qu'il devrait sélectionner dans tel ou tel contexte. La TCR peut ainsi devenir scientifiquement utile et générer un programme de recherche en économie, en sociologie ou en science politique. L'économie expérimentale, dès ses débuts dans les années 1950, indique toutefois que la TCR, ou du moins les hypothèses auxiliaires qu'elles s'étaient adjointes, ne sont pas vérifiées. Aversion au risque et à l'incertitude, violation de l'axiome d'indépendance, préférences pour des solutions moralement préférables mais économiquement suboptimales ; la liste des dissonances est longue.

Plutôt que de considérer que la TCR avait été falsifiée, la théorie économique, l'épistémologie des sciences sociales et la philosophie de l'action ont généralement opté, relativement au fossé entre la théorie et les faits, pour une des trois attitudes suivantes, que nous nommerons *téléologisme*, *instrumentalisme*, et *interprétativisme*. (Cette nomenclature ne vise pas à départager les auteurs, mais plutôt les arguments employés pour faire face au fossé entre la théorie et les données expérimentales.)

Selon la première (téléologiste), des agents situés suffisamment longtemps dans une dynamique de marché finiront par adopter les prescriptions de la TCR. S'ils ne le font pas, ils seront éliminés. En d'autres mots, le marché finira par sélectionner les individus et firmes rationnelles. La TCR décrit donc un ensemble de règles que les agents tendront à adopter. L'apprentissage et l'évolution du marché interagissent de façon à maintenir les agents sur la voie de la rationalité. Les expériences qui mettent à jour l'irrationalité des agents ne font que souligner les imperfections propres aux débutants ou non-experts.

Selon la seconde interprétation (instrumentaliste), la TCR ne décrit pas le comportement d'agents réels, mais d'agents idéaux. Elle construit des modèles mathématiques de la prise de décision, des modèles « sans friction », dans lesquels on ne tient pas compte des erreurs (de calcul, de temps, d'information) et des limitations des agents. L'agent idéal occupe, épistémologiquement parlant, le même rôle que le gaz idéal ou la lentille parfaite. Comme Friedman et Savage [1948, p. 298] le soulignent, on pourrait prédire adéquatement le comportement d'un joueur professionnel de billard si on pouvait calculer, à l'aide de formules physiques, les différentes trajectoires possibles et évaluer les plus profitables. On fait l'hypothèse que le joueur se comporte « comme si » il connaissait les formules et pouvait estimer les angles et calculer les trajectoires. La science économique, selon Friedman [1953], n'a pas d'engagement ontologique et ses entités ne sont que des paramètres dans le calcul économique. Les expériences montrent certes que des agents réels ne sont pas des *Homo oeconomicus*, mais cela n'est pas plus surprenant que d'apprendre qu'un gaz réel ne se comporte pas complètement comme un gaz idéal. L'important est, en bout de ligne, le caractère prédictif du modèle.

Selon la troisième attitude (interprétativiste), la rationalité est une norme d'interprétation du comportement qui permet la compréhension d'autrui ; la TCR y joue un rôle périphérique [voir par exemple Davidson 1993]. Même si les agents ne se conforment pas à la TCR, ils sont toujours interprétables comme étant motivés par des raisons. La rationalité des agents est constitutive d'un ensemble de principes interprétatifs plutôt que de règles explicites. Bien qu'on puisse codifier des normes d'inférence et de décision (logique, théorie bayesienne du choix rationnel, théorie des jeux, etc.), il n'y a pas de principes universels qui nous permettent de répondre univoquement à des question comme « que croire ? », « quelle croyance réviser ? » ou « que faire ? », ou encore des principes qui nous permettent d'interpréter univoquement le comportement d'une personne. Un agent qui agit ou qui interprète a toujours le choix entre réviser une croyance locale ou une théorie générale, de sorte que la bonne croyance ou la bonne action ne peut pas être déduite des modèles théoriques. Le holisme des croyances rend caduque toute tentative d'expliciter les normes d'interprétations du comportement. Ne demeurent alors que des principes généraux et constitutifs : attribuer une activité mentale, une rationalité, des croyances, des désirs, des connaissances, etc. Les théories de la rationalité sont des connaissances d'arrière-plan qui nous servent à interpréter le comportement plutôt qu'à le produire. Elles proposent des normes épistémiques et pratiques d'utilisation des concepts de croyances, désirs, action et rationalité. Les expériences démontrent non pas l'irrationalité des agents, mais plutôt que les raisons qui motivent ceux-ci ne sont pas conformes aux théories codifiées. Bien que techniquement irrationnels, les sujets sont toujours interprétables comme des agents rationnels.

## 2. Quand le formalisme mène au normativisme

Derrière ces trois interprétations se cache le même arrière-plan épistémologique que nous nommerons le normativisme, à savoir l'idée selon laquelle une théorie de la rationalité est essentiellement une théorie normative. Cet arrière-plan a largement modulé le rapport entre les théories formelles de la décision et les résultats expérimentaux. Nous illustrerons cette relation à l'aide d'un exemple en particulier, soit le jeu de l'ultimatum [*cf.* Camerer 2003].

Dans l'ultimatum, un agent A doit proposer une fraction $f > 0$, de son choix, d'un montant $m$ d'argent à un agent B. Si B accepte, B reçoit $f$, et A empoche $m-f$. Si B refuse, personne ne touche un sou. L'interprétation standard de la théorie des jeux prédit que les agents se comporteront comme suit : A proposera la plus petite fraction possible, et B acceptera n'importe quel montant. Or les données expérimentales montrent que les agents A proposent des montants représentant en moyenne 20 à 50 % du butin, et les agents B refusent généralement les montants inférieurs à 20 ou 30 %. Le résultat est robuste peu importe le montant d'argent, la culture, le degré d'anonymat, l'expérience, etc. Les seuls cas où les agents se comportent approximativement de façon conforme à l'interprétation standard sont ceux où B (mais non A) est un ordinateur et où A et B sont des groupes qui prennent des décisions collectives.

On peut donc appliquer les trois interprétations de la TCR à ces résultats :

– Téléologisme : si les agents jouent de façon répétée à l'ultimatum, ils finiront par adopter la stratégie optimale ; les offres seront aussi minimes que possible, et toute offre sera acceptée.

– Instrumentalisme : si les agents ne suivent pas une stratégie optimale, cela est dû à leur imperfection ; généralement, la théorie fournit néanmoins des prédictions utiles.

– Interprétativisme : on peut interpréter les sujets comme ayant des raisons de sélectionner des stratégies suboptimales ; par exemple, ils valorisent l'équité ou encore l'absence de risque.

Implicitement, chacune de ces interprétations tend vers la même idée : une théorie de la rationalité est essentiellement une théorie des normes de la rationalité, lesquelles se réduisent soit aux règles qu'un agent rationnel finira par suivre (téléologisme), soit à celles que suivrait un agent idéal (instrumentalisme), soit à celles par lesquelles nous interprétons un agent rationnel (interprétativisme). L'idée selon laquelle une théorie de la rationalité est une théorie normative est ancrée dans la pratique philosophique et économique au point où, lorsque des expériences ont montré que les agents ne se comportaient pas comme la théorie le prédisait, on a préféré parler de « paradoxes » (d'Allais, d'Ellsberg, etc.) plutôt que de réfutations empiriques ou de contre-exemples, marquant par là le caractère non seulement logique et formel, mais également normatif de ces théories.

Les perspectives normativistes mettent cependant la TCR dans une position épistémologiquement problématique. En effet, le téléologisme et l'instrumentalisme tiennent pour acquis l'utilité de la TCR : que ce soit en tant que finalité ou en tant qu'abstraction pratique, elle décrit toujours un état idéal des agents rationnels, et cet idéal n'est pas sujet à la réfutation. Des théorèmes et des axiomatiques démontrent formellement l'issue rationnelle des jeux : la validité de la TCR ne s'évalue pas à l'aune de ses prédictions, mais de ses vertus formelles (complétude, consistance, etc.). Si, dans le jeu de l'ultimatum, les sujets font des offres irrationnelles (plus que le minimum) et refusent des offres non nulles, ce n'est pas parce que la théorie prédit mal, mais parce que les agents démontrent des biais irrationnels. *Augmentez les montants, et vous verrez qu'ils adopteront des stratégies optimales*, affirmaient les économistes sceptiques devant les résultats expérimentaux de l'ultimatum. Or, dans une version où les joueurs devaient partager un montant de 100 $, même des offres de 30 $ faisaient l'objet d'un refus [Camerer et Thaler 1995]. Si la TCR décrit une finalité ou un idéal de rationalité, on peut certainement exiger que cette finalité et cet idéal soient justifiés.

L'argumentaire justifiant les normes de rationalité va généralement comme suit : tout comme la grammaire est constituée de normes linguistiques, les théories de la rationalité sont constituées de normes de décision qui recommandent des cours d'action. La TCR est « un ensemble consistant de normes, et non une étude empirique » [Marschak 1951, p. 13]. Si une personne ne choisit pas ce que la TCR recommande, elle commet une erreur. De même, si une personne se trompe en multipliant 234 par 92, ce n'est pas l'arithmétique qui est en faute, mais la personne. Cette dernière *devrait* trouver 21 528. L'économie théorique n'est pas alors une science susceptible de formuler des propositions falsifiables, mais de décrire comment les agents économiques se comporteraient s'ils étaient des individus complètement rationnels. Les proposeurs *devraient* offrir des montants minimaux et les receveurs *devraient* accepter toute proposition. Une pratique n'est rationnelle que si elle peut être rationalisée à l'intérieur du modèle théorique. Ce faisant, cependant, la théorie s'exclut elle-même, en grande partie, du champ scientifique puisque la science s'efforce de procéder à une tentative systématique de vérification, falsification et comparaison des théories. Elle n'est dès lors qu'une tautologie complexe, justifiée par sa rigueur formelle.

L'interprétativisme, au fond, ne fais qu'expliciter ce point de vue : la rationalité ne s'analyse pas en règles et en codifications, mais en principes d'interprétation. L'agent idéal est tout simplement représenté autrement que par la TCR. Popper disait ainsi du principe de rationalité qu'il s'agissait d'un principe « quasiment vide » [1985, p. 359]. La théorie de la rationalité oscille donc entre tautologie et banalité. Dans la prochaine section, nous nous intéressons à deux manières de contourner les difficultés relatives au normativisme : la première est proposée par l'économie expérimentale et la seconde par la neuroéconomie.

## 3. RÉCONCILIER LE FORMEL ET LE CAUSAL : UNE VISION MÉCANISTE DE L'UTILITÉ

Une manière de contourner les difficultés reliées au normativisme est d'abandonner les hypothèses auxiliaires mentionnées plus haut : le postulat de rationalité et l'attribution d'une fonction d'utilité égoïste. C'est historiquement ce qu'a choisi de faire l'économie expérimentale. Ce faisant, elle renverse cependant l'objet de la recherche économique : il ne s'agit plus de prédire le comportement des agents, mais bien de partir de ces comportements pour découvrir des biais cognitifs ou explorer des fonctions d'utilité. Le programme de recherche de Tversky et Kahneman, par exemple, ne porte plus sur la prédiction de l'action, mais sur la manière dont l'action révèle des biais cognitifs [Kahneman *et alii* 1982]. Les recherches conduites par Werner Güth, Ernst Fehr, Frans van Winden, Georgre Ainslie et d'autres économistes expérimentaux, quant à elles, visent à utiliser les décisions réelles des acteurs pour décrire d'une manière plus précise leur fonction d'utilité (en tenant compte, par exemple, de l'aspect dynamique des préférences ou de l'existence de préférences sociales). Ce renversement est semblable à celui mis de l'avant dans l'analyse des préférences révélées, utilisée pour interpréter le comportement des consommateurs [Samuelson 1938]. Cette analyse ne cherchait plus à prédire le comportement des agents à partir d'une fonction d'utilité hypothétique, mais à explorer la fonction d'utilité des agents en observant leurs choix réels.

Grâce à l'économie expérimentale, la TCR peut s'adjoindre des hypothèses auxiliaires plus précises que celles associées à son interprétation standard. Dans le jeu de l'ultimatum, par exemple, le rejet des offres jugées insuffisantes justifie l'ajout de préférences sociales à la fonction d'utilité égoïste. L'économiste expérimental peut ainsi mesurer l'utilité associée au rejet de l'offre injuste, qui s'élèvera à 20 %-30 % du total pour la plupart des joueurs. Même avec l'ajout de l'économie expérimentale, la TCR demeure toutefois une théorie formelle sans ancrage causal. Les entrées (perceptions) y sont reliées aux sorties (actions) par une fonction d'utilité (qui attribue une valeur aux états du monde) et par des mécanismes formels qui ordonnent les préférences.

Ce modèle formel, revu à la lumière des données empiriques, peut à son tour se transformer en modèle normatif, mais il peut également éviter ce piège. Pour ce faire, il doit chercher à relier les mécanismes formels à des processus et des structures causalement impliqués dans le contrôle de l'action. Les neurosciences (et en particulier la « neuroéconomie, » soit les neurosciences de la décision) ont ainsi suggéré que la prise de décision est le produit de plusieurs mécanismes distincts d'évaluation, de motivation et de sélection de l'action. Bien qu'encore à leurs balbutiements, ces domaines sont déjà à même de nous fournir des modèles causaux précisant la nature de la décision économique.

Dans plusieurs cas, les neurosciences ne font que confirmer nos intuitions, en montrant que des processus que nous concevons comme distincts sont effectivement réalisés dans des structures et des processus distincts. Dans d'autres, cependant, elles nous encouragent à affirmer (ou à réaffirmer) des distinctions négligées par les modèles formels en théorie de la décision. Une des trouvailles suggérant une telle révision est la découverte d'une dissociation entre l'appréciation (*liking*) et la motivation (*wanting*). Les recherches en neuroscience de Berridge et de ses collègues, par exemple, montrent que les systèmes dopaminergiques – un ensemble de structures sous-corticales, majoritairement situées dans l'aire tegmentale ventrale – sont en grande partie responsables de la motivation. L'activité de ces neurones est nécessaire pour que les indices reliés à des récompenses acquièrent une signification et une saillance motivationnelle. Des souris et des rats génétiquement modifiés afin de ne plus produire de dopamine perdent la *motivation* à acquérir de la nourriture sans pour autant cesser de *l'apprécier*. Ils manifestent par exemple tous les signes externes typiques de l'appréciation du sucre ou de la nourriture (ils passent la langue sur leurs lèvres), mais ne démontrent aucune motivation à ingérer du sucre ou toute autre nourriture auquel l'animal est sensible normalement [Berridge et Robinson 1998]. Le même phénomène a été constaté chez l'humain. Par exemple des fumeurs à qui on administre un antagoniste de la dopamine éprouvent le même plaisir à fumer sans pourtant en avoir le désir [Berridge et Robinson 2003]. Ces recherches suggèrent que la motivation n'est pas en premier lieu la recherche d'un stimulus agréable, mais la recherche de ressources, et que cette motivation est le produit des systèmes dopaminergiques. La distinction neuro-psychologique entre la motivation et l'appréciation nous rapproche d'une explication causale de la relation entre l'utilité et l'action.

Une autre des trouvailles de la neuroéconomie est que le concept d'appréciation ne correspond pas à un seul mécanisme, mais à plusieurs. Dans un premier temps, on peut distinguer l'appréciation *primaire* de l'appréciation *secondaire*. L'appréciation primaire est une évaluation du caractère hédonique (l'intensité et la valence) de certains stimuli. Elle s'incarne elle-même dans plus d'une structure. On sait par exemple que le nucleus accumbens est impliqué dans la *récompense* (appréciation primaire positive) alors que l'insula est impliquée dans la *punition* (appréciation primaire négative). Des stimuli plaisants (nourriture, drogue, etc.) suscitent l'activité du premier, alors que des stimuli répulsifs ou dégoûtants (comme, par exemple, de la nourriture avariée) suscitent celle du deuxième [Sprengelmeyer 2007; Berridge et Robinson 2003]. De même, l'amygdale est principalement impliquée dans les réponses au danger (peur, panique, etc.).

Apprécier un stimulus comme étant plaisant ou déplaisant est donc distinct de la motivation, mais aussi de ce qu'on peut appeler l'appréciation secondaire. Sans elle, il nous serait sans doute impossible de construire ce que les modèles formels présentent comme des préférences. En effet, préférer A à B implique que, si on fait la somme des coûts et bénéfices, A se révèle supérieur. Des aires préfrontales, comme le cortex orbitofrontal et le cortex préfrontal ventromédian, intègrent les inputs en provenance des aires d'appréciation primaires [Wallis 2007; Rushworth *et alii* 2007]. Dans des situations de prises de décision, on considère que ces aires encodent la valeur économique, la valeur des buts ou encore la disposition à acheter (*willingness to pay*). Dans une expérience de Plassmann et ses collègues [2007], où des sujets affamés doivent décider de la valeur économique d'un plat, l'activation du cortex orbitofrontal est proportionnelle à la valeur que les sujets attribuent au stimulus. Les études de lésions cérébrales par Damasio et ses collaborateurs illustrent la différence – et les relations complexes – entre l'appréciation primaire et secondaire. Au Jeu de l'Iowa, des participants doivent piger des cartes parmi un choix de 4 paquets, dont les taux de paiement et de punition varient considérablement (les sujets sont informés de la valeur de leur gain ou de leur perte immédiatement après la sélection d'une carte). Des sujets normaux arrivent rapidement à identifier les paquets profitables et à éviter les autres. Damasio [2000] a montré que le comportement des sujets s'accompagne de réactions physiologiques – telles qu'un accroissement de la conductance de la peau – qui surviennent à la fois lorsqu'ils apprennent la valeur de leur carte et lorsqu'ils anticipent cette valeur. Des patients victimes de lésions au cortex orbitrofrontal ou au cortex préfrontal ventromedian manifestent des réactions physiologiques uniquement lorsqu'ils apprennent la valeur de leur carte mais non pas lorsqu'ils l'anticipent. Ils sont donc incapables de développer une appréciation secondaire, c'est-à-dire une préférence pour une option, et sont condamnés à expérimenter, après coup, la valeur de leur choix. On pourrait donc dire, en termes neuronaux, que la formation des préférences exige l'intégration des aires d'appréciation primaire et secondaire.

Finalement, outre la motivation, l'appréciation primaire et l'appréciation secondaire, on peut identifier une troisième forme d'appréciation dite *cognitive*. Des aires préfrontales (en particulier la partie gauche du cortex dorsolatéral préfrontal, CDLPF) permettent de maintenir l'attention sur des buts non hédoniques et non émotifs, mais davantage intellectuels. Il peut s'agir, par exemple, d'acquérir de l'argent, de poursuivre un but pré-sélectionné ou de se conformer à des normes sociales. Dans chaque cas, l'issue du processus de décision est déterminée par une valeur qui n'est pas (ou pas nécessairement) associée à des stimuli agréables. Cette caractéristique structurelle du système de prise de décision permet d'expliquer la distinction – absente de l'appareil conceptuel de la TCR classique mais omniprésente dans le langage courant – entre l'utile et l'agréable [Jackendoff 2007, p. 283-284]. L'agréable réfère avant tout aux situations ou événements qui activent les aires d'appréciation primaire et secondaire, alors que l'utile désigne les situations ou événements qui mènent à des appréciations cognitives. Si nous apprécions l'argent, par exemple, c'est parce que nous la trouvons utile. Or nous la trouvons utile parce que nous en faisons un moyen pour acquérir des biens ou des services qui permettront à leur tour d'accéder à des stimuli plaisants.

Les structures sous-jacentes au concept d'appréciation cognitive nous permettent par ailleurs d'expliquer de manière causale ce que plusieurs théories de l'utilité ont déjà modélisé sur le plan formel. La picoéconomie de George Ainslie [1992], par exemple, a bien mis en évidence comment nos fonctions d'utilité variaient avec le temps et comment notre capacité à différer une récompense était déterminante dans le processus décisionnel. Cela coïncide avec le fait que le développement des aires préfrontales chez l'enfant lui permet de poursuivre des buts plus abstraits en inhibant, par exemple, une récompense immédiate pour obtenir une récompense à long terme. Un des principaux défis de la neuroéconomie au cours des années à venir consistera à décrire de manière plus détaillée les mécanismes impliqués dans la poursuite des buts cognitifs. Même si les aires préfrontales sont généralement reconnues comme le siège des processus de contrôle cognitif de haut niveau, il n'existe malheureusement pas une théorie unique quant à leur fonctionnement [Jurado et Rosselli 2007]. Au minimum, on doit supposer l'existence de mécanismes permettant 1) le contrôle de l'attention, 2) la planification des actions complexes et 3) l'inhibition des actions ou des stimuli non pertinents, mais nous sommes encore dans l'attente d'un modèle qui intègrera d'une manière cohérente les données psychologiques et neurologiques. Or un tel modèle permettra de décrire avec beaucoup plus de précision le processus décisionnel.

Quoi qu'il en soit, la neuroéconomie permet déjà d'atteindre une conception plus raffinée de l'appréciation que celle généralement favorisée dans les théories normatives sous le concept d'utilité. Les distinctions que nous avons esquissées peuvent être rapprochées de celles proposées par Kahneman et ses collègues [1997] entre les différents types d'utilité. *L'utilité de la décision*, au sens classique, est assimilée à l'activité motivationnelle des neurones dopaminergique : c'est elle qui est révélée par la décision de faire X. Elle peut toutefois être distinguée de l'utilité *expérimentée* (l'appréciation de X pendant la décision), de l'utilité *prédite* (l'appréciation de X avant la décision) et de l'utilité *remémorée* (l'appréciation de X après la décision). Cette typologie permet d'ajouter de la substance à la thèse de la maximisation de l'utilité. Elle fournit également un schéma qui fait le pont entre les données neuronales et les données comportementales, tout en mettant en relation les aspects formels de la théorie de la rationalité avec des mécanismes causaux.

Ce schéma permet d'expliquer, par exemple, comment un comportement peut révéler des préférences (motivation/utilité classique) sans pour autant que ces préférences ne soient reflétées dans l'utilité prédite (l'appréciation avant la décision). Ou encore, comment l'utilité prédite peut être cognitive sans être hédonique, c'est-à-dire comment une chose une peut-être utile sans être agréable. De même, la préférence – en tant qu'appréciation secondaire survenant *avant* la décision – peut être cohérente ou non avec l'utilité de la décision : la cohérence en question sera une question de fait plutôt que de définition. Sans se substituer aux mécanismes formels décrits par l'économie expérimentale, la neuroéconomie laisse donc entrevoir la possibilité d'une description mécaniste et causale de la prise de décision rationnelle.

## 4. La mécanique de la décision : deux exemples

Nous avons soutenu jusqu'à présent que la neuroéconomie permettait de réconcilier une analyse formelle de la décision avec une analyse causale. Les modèles neuroéconomiques permettent ainsi de conserver le formalisme de la TCR, mais en ancrant le processus de décision dans des structures et des processus neuronaux (en somme, des *mécanismes*). Les concepts d'utilité, de sélection de l'action ou de préférence acquièrent ainsi une définition plus précise et une signification causale. Donnons-en une illustration à partir de deux exemples concrets : 1) la décision d'acheter et 2) le jeu de l'ultimatum.

Knutson et ses collègues [2007] ont présenté à des sujets l'image d'un produit attrayant (du chocolat Godiva) en leur laissant 4 secondes pour décider s'ils souhaitaient acquérir ce produit. Ensuite, ils affichaient le prix du produit (parfois bas, parfois élevé) et demandaient aux sujets de décider s'ils voulaient ou non acheter le produit à ce prix. Évidemment, les sujets refusaient d'acheter les produits dont le prix était trop élevé (80 $ pour une boîte de chocolat) et préféraient les produits dont le prix était généralement bas (7 $ pour la même boîte). L'intérêt de l'expérience se situe sur le plan neuropsychologique. Lorsqu'on demande aux sujets s'ils souhaitent acheter, les produits désirables provoquent une activation du nucleus accumbens, cette région du cerveau associée au plaisir et à l'anticipation des récompenses. En revanche, lorsque le prix est affiché, on détecte une activation de l'insula, une région associée à la douleur, au dégoût et aux autres émotions négatives. L'activation est moindre lorsque le prix est jugé acceptable, auquel cas les structures préfrontales, impliquées dans la planification et le contrôle, sont également sollicitées. Sur le plan causal, l'activation de ces régions permet de prédire de manière efficace si le sujet achètera ou non le produit : l'activation préfrontale permet de prédire l'achat, alors qu'une forte activation insulaire permet de prédire le refus du produit [Knutson *et alii* 2007]. En somme, on explique la décision comme un compromis, où les aires préfrontales jouent le rôle de médiateur, entre le plaisir d'acquérir, manifeste dans l'activation du nucleus accumbens, et le désagrément relié à l'achat qui se manifeste dans l'insula. L'analyse permet d'illustrer comment la fonction d'utilité de l'acheteur est en fait déterminée par l'activation de structures neuronales concrètes. Elle permet également d'expliquer des caractéristiques bien connues du processus de décision. Par exemple, le fait que le temps de décision soit plus rapide pour les prix très élevés et très bas que pour les prix intermédiaires. La différence dans le temps de décision s'explique en effet par la nécessité de faire intervenir les aires préfrontales pour résoudre le conflit entre l'insula (déplaisir) et le nucleus accumbens (le plaisir).

Une deuxième série d'études digne de mention est celle reliée au jeu de l'ultimatum. Les études d'imageries fonctionnelles révèlent que l'insula antérieure, le cortex préfrontal dorsolatéral – lié au contrôle cognitif et à l'attention – et le cortex antérieur cingulé – lié au conflit cognitif, la détection des erreurs et la modulation émotive – sont activés au moment d'accepter ou de rejeter une offre [Sanfey *et alii* 2003]. Une offre perçue comme insuffisante déclenche dans le cerveau des répondeurs un sentiment de « dégoût » : plus les offres sont jugées insuffisantes, plus l'activation de l'insula antérieure est intense. Cette réaction affective n'est pas uniquement une réponse à une récompense monétaire jugée insuffisante, puisque l'activation est sensiblement inférieure quand le proposeur est un ordinateur. Ainsi, le fait d'être déçu par un humain nous dégoûte davantage que de l'être par un ordinateur.

Quand une offre est jugé suffisante, il semble normal de l'accepter : il y a un gain monétaire et aucun sentiment négatif. Quand l'offre est insuffisante, cependant, le cerveau fait face à un dilemme : punir le proposeur injuste, ou obtenir un peu d'argent ? La décision finale dépend du poids respectif de l'activation du CDLPF et de l'insula antérieure. L'activation de l'insula antérieure est donc corrélée à la fois au degré d'insuffisance et à la décision de rejeter des offres insuffisante [Sanfey *et alii* 2003, p. 1756]. Le cortex antérieur cingulé, plus actif quand les offres sont insuffisantes, se comporte comme un modérateur entre le but cognitif (le désir d'obtenir plus d'argent) et le but émotif (le désir de punir). Ainsi, les sujets réagissent de manière viscérale à l'incapacité des autres de répondre à leurs attentes. Les données neuroéconomiques sont également confirmées par les données physiologiques et celles tirées de l'introspection. L'activation de l'insula antérieure, par exemple, est corrélée avec les changements physiologiques associés à l'émotion de colère, comme une plus grande conductance de la peau [van't Wout *et alii* 2006], et les sujets interprètent leur réaction émotionnelle comme telle [Ben-Shakhar 2007].

Les offres insuffisantes suscitent donc une réponse émotive forte. Mais le comportement ne se réduit pas à une simple réponse affective primaire, puisque des mécanismes cognitifs de haut niveau interviennent également dans le contrôle de l'action. Par exemple, d'autres études ont montré comment la partie droite du CDLPF (et non la gauche), lorsqu'on perturbe artificiellement son fonctionnement à l'aide de stimulation magnétique transcranienne (SMT), parvient moins efficacement à moduler le comportement : les sujets soumis à la SMT, plutôt que de rejeter les offres insuffisantes comme à l'habitude, acceptent toutes les offres possibles [Knoch *et alii* 2006]. Curieusement, ils acceptent ces offres bien qu'ils les considèrent toujours insuffisantes. Or on sait que le CDLPF droit est très largement associé à l'inhibition des réponses prédominantes. Lorsqu'on trouble son fonctionnement, il devient plus difficile pour les sujets de résister à la tentation. Les sujets deviennent également plus susceptibles de s'engager dans des comportements risqués [Knoch et Fehr 2007].

Une autre aire essentielle pour comprendre le fonctionnement de la décision dans les jeux de l'ultimatum est le cortex préfrontal ventromédian (CPFVM). Lorsqu'il est affecté (chez les patients cérébro-lésés), les sujets rejettent plus facilement les offres insuffisantes [Koenigs et Tranel 2007]. La compréhension du fonctionnement du CPFVM demeure l'un des grands défis de la neuroéconomie. Par exemple, les mêmes patients cérébraux-lésés, lorsqu'ils font face à des dilemmes moraux complexes, ont tendance à adopter davantage des raisonnements utilitaristes que les patients normaux, ce qui peut laisser croire qu'ils contrôlent davantage leurs émotions ou qu'ils sont moins émotifs [Koenigs *et alii* 2007]. Comment une même lésion peut-elle rendre les gens plus émotifs dans un cas (le jeu de l'ultimatum) et moins dans un autre (les dilemmes moraux complexes) ? Une réponse possible est que le CPFVM permet à la fois la prise en considération des gains futurs et la modulation des émotions typiquement sociales (la sympathie et la détresse face au malheur d'autrui) mais non d'émotions négatives élémentaires comme la colère [Moll and de Oliveira-Souza 2007]. Ainsi, le dysfonctionnement du CPFVM rendrait plus difficile la prise en considération des gains futurs (dans le jeu de l'ultimatum), tout en facilitant les jugements utilitaristes. Bien qu'incomplètes, les recherches sur le CPFVM démontrent l'intérêt de la neuroéconomie pour l'étude de la rationalité, que ce soit au plan formel ou causal. Plutôt que d'opposer trop simplement les mécanismes d'appréciation et de contrôle (les émotions et la cognition), elles nous rappellent l'importance dans la prise de décision des mécanismes d'intégration des émotions et des risques, de même que leur interaction avec les stimuli sociaux.

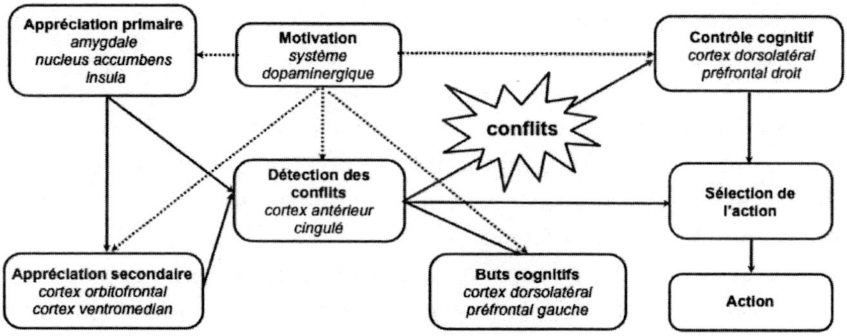


Figure 1
Principaux mécanismes neuroéconomiques de décision

## CONCLUSION

Selon la définition classique de Lionel Robbins, l'économie est la « science qui étudie les comportements humains en tant que relation entre les fins et les moyens rares à usages alternatifs » [Robbins 1932, p. 13]. On peut comprendre cette relation entre les moyens et les fins comme une relation formelle, ou une relation causale. Dans le présent article, nous avons soutenu que la théorie du choix rationnel, dans son interprétation standard, se présente comme une théorie formelle, négligeant l'analyse causale et adoptant une attitude normative. L'économie expérimentale permet de résoudre une partie du problème, en rompant avec l'approche normative et en remplaçant les hypothèses sous-jacentes à l'interprétation standard de la TCR par des hypothèses plus réalistes sur la prise de décision rationnelle. L'attribution d'une fonction d'utilité qui inclut des préférences sociales, par exemple, permet d'améliorer la prédictivité de la théorie dans des jeux comme celui de l'ultimatum. L'économie expérimentale ne parvient pas cependant à surmonter une autre difficulté théorique à laquelle fait face la TCR, à savoir la nature formelle des entités postulées. Nous avons montré comment la neuroéconomie, parce que son étude ne se limite pas aux des manifestations comportementales, laisse entrevoir le développement d'une véritable science naturelle de la décision. Cette science postulerait des mécanismes fortement inspirés des processus neuronaux et proposerait des modélisations se rapprochant davantage des neurosciences computationnelles que de la logique. Cette théorie offrirait un modèle descriptif de la prise de décision. L'optimalité, dans ce cas, ne serait pas dérivé des axiomes de la TCR, mais plutôt présentée comme l'effet de mécanismes neurologiques de contrôle de l'action, évalués dans un environnement de référence.

De la sorte, le rapprochement entre la biologie et l'économie, inauguré entre autres par Darwin, pourra trouver son expression dans une science générale de « l'économie de la nature ».

## RÉFÉRENCES

AINSLIE G., 1992, *Picoeconomics: The strategic interaction of successive motivational states within the person*, Cambridge, Cambridge UP.

BEN-SHAKAR G., BORNSTEIN G., HOPFENSITZ A. and VAN WINDEN F., 2007, « Reciprocity and emotions in bargaining: Using physiological and self-report measures », *Journal of Economic Psychology*, 28(3), p. 314-323.

BERRIDGE K.C. and ROBINSON T.E., 1998, "What is the role of dopamine in reward: Hedonic impact, reward learning, or incentive salience?", *Brain Research Reviews*, 28(3), p. 309-369.

–, 2003, "Parsing reward", *Trends in Neuroscience*, 26(9), p. 507-513.

BINMORE K., 1994, "Rationality in the Centipede", *in* R. Fagin (ed.), *Theoretical Aspects of Reasoning About Knowledge: Proceedings of the 5th Conference (Tark 1994)*, San Francisco (CA), Kaufmann, p. 150-159.

CAMERER C., 2003, *Behavioral game theory: Experiments in strategic interaction*, Princeton, Princeton UP.

— and THALER R.H., 1995, "Anomalies: Ultimatums, Dictators and Manners", *The Journal of Economic Perspectives*, 9(2), p. 209-219.

DAMASIO A., 2000, *L'Erreur de Descartes*, Paris, Odile Jacob.

DAVIDSON D., 1993, *Actions et événements*, Paris, PUF.

FRIEDMAN M., 1953, *Essays in Positive Economics*, Chicago, University of Chicago Press.

— and SAVAGE L.J., 1948, "The Utility Analysis of Choices Involving Risk", *Journal of Political Economy*, 56, p. 279-304.

JACKENDOFF R., 2007, *Language, consciousness, culture: Essays on mental structures*, Cambridge (Mass.), MIT Press.

JURADO M.B. and ROSSELLI M., 2007, "The elusive nature of executive functions: A review of our current understanding", *Neuropsychological review*, 17(3), p. 213-233.

KAHNEMAN D., SLOVIC P. and TVERSKY A., 1982, *Judgment under uncertainty: Heuristics and biases*, Cambridge, Cambridge UP.

KAHNEMAN D., WAKKER P.P. and SARIN R., 1997, "Back to Bentham? Explorations of experienced utility", *The Quarterly Journal of Economics*, 112(2), p. 375-405.

KNOCH D. and FEHR E., 2007, "Resisting the power of temptations: The right prefrontal cortex and self-control", *Annals of the New York Academy of Sciences*, 1104, p. 123-134.

—, PASCUAL-LEONE A., MEYER K., TREYER V. and FEHR E., 2006, "Diminishing reciprocal fairness by disrupting the right prefrontal cortex", *Science*, 314(5800), p. 829-832.

KNUTSON B., RICK S., WIMMER G.E., PRELEC D. and LOEWENSTEIN G., 2007, "Neural predictors of purchases", *Neuron*, 53(1), p. 147-156.

KOENIGS M. and TRANEL D., 2007, "Irrational economic decision-making after ventromedial prefrontal damage: Evidence from the ultimatum game", *Journal of Neuroscience*, 27(4), p. 951-956.

—, YOUNG L., ADOLPHS R., TRANEL D., CUSHMAN F., HAUSER M. and DAMASIO A., 2007, "Damage to the prefrontal cortex increases utilitarian moral judgements", *Nature*, 446, p. 908-911.

MARSCHAK J., 1951, *Why "Should" Statisticians and Businessmen Maximize "Moral Expectation"?*, Paper presented at the Second Berkeley Symposium on Mathematical Statistics and Probability, Cowles Foundation Paper 53.

MOLL J. and DE OLIVEIRA-SOUZA R., 2007, "Moral judgments, emotions and the utilitarian brain", *Trends in Cognitive Sciences*, 11(8), p. 319-321.

PLASSMANN H., O'DOHERTY J. and RANGEL A., 2007, "Orbitofrontal cortex encodes willingness to pay in everyday economic transactions", *Journal of Neuroscience*, 27(37), p. 9984-9988.

POPPER K., 1985, "The rationality principle", *in* D. Miller (ed.), *Popper selections*, Princeton, Princeton UP.

ROBBINS L., 1932, *An essay on the nature and signifiance of economic science*, London, Macmillan.

RUSHWORTH M., BEHRENS T., RUDEBECK P. and WALTON M., 2007, "Contrasting roles for cingulate and orbitofrontal cortex in decisions and social behaviour", *Trends in Cognitive Sciences*, 11(4), p. 168-176.

SAMUELSON P., 1938, "A note on the pure theory of consumers' behaviour", *Economica*, 5, p. 61-71.

SANFEY A.G., RILLING J.K., ARONSON J.A., NYSTROM L.E. and COHEN J.D., 2003, "The neural basis of economic decision-making in the ultimatum game", *Science*, 300(5626), p. 1755-1758.

SAVAGE L.J., 1954, *The foundations of statistics*, New York, J. Wiley.

SPRENGELMEYER R., 2007, "The neurology of disgust", *Brain*, 130(7), p. 1715-1717.

VAN'T WOUT M., KAHN R.S., SANFEY A.G. and ALEMAN A., 2006, "Affective state and decision-making in the ultimatum game", *Experimental Brain Research*, 169(4), p. 564-568.

WALLIS J.D., 2007, "Orbitofrontal cortex and its contribution to decision-making", *Annual Review of Neuroscience*, 30, p. 31-56.

# CONSENT, CONTESTABILITY AND EMPLOYER AUTHORITY

LARS LINDBLOM*

**Résumé**
Cet article discute l'argument selon lequel l'autorité de l'employeur se légitime par le consentement des employés. Si l'analyse économique contemporaine des contrats de travail est correcte, alors nous devons, pour expliquer l'existence de contrats de travail, faire l'hypothèse que les parties qui le signent essaient de réduire leur incertitude ou leur ignorance en prévision de décisions à prendre. C'est pourquoi les parties sont d'accord pour signer un contrat incomplet dans lequel l'employeur à l'autorité. Cependant, ceci implique que le consentement a été donné sous des conditions d'ignorance. Il en découle alors que les décisions prises par l'employeur ne peuvent pas être justifiées par le consentement parce que l'ignorance empêche de satisfaire le critère selon lequel le consentement ne peut être le fait que d'individus informés. Il faut donc trouver une autre légitimation à l'autorité des employeurs sur les employés. Nous suggérons que les actes d'autorité ne peuvent être légitimes que si les employés ont de réelles possibilités pour les contester.
**Mots-clés** : contestabilité, consentement, ignorance, contrats incomplets, contrats de travail

**Abstract**
A common idea is that market exchange is justified by informed and free agreement between parties. This paper investigates the

* Lecturer at the Royal Institute of Technology, Division of Philosophy, Teknikringen 78b, SE-100 44 Stockholm, Sweden, lars.lindblom@infra.kth.se.

idea that employer authority is justified by consent. According to this view, agents in the market are informed of the consequences of their actions and are not coerced. This makes their acts voluntary. A problem in the application of this justification to the employer/employee relationship is pointed out If the contemporary economics of the employment contracts is correct, we must, in order to explain the existence of such contracts, make the assumption that the contracting parties are attempting to deal with decision-theoretic ignorance. This is why the parties agree to an incomplete contract in which the employer has authority. However, this implies that consent to acts of authority has been given under conditions of ignorance; it follows, then, that the course of action that the employer chooses to take cannot be justified by consent because the informedness criterion of consent will not have been satisfied due to this ignorance. Another method of justification must be sought. It is suggested that in order to achieve justification of acts of authority, there should be in place a real possibility to contest employers' decisions. This possibility is needed, rather than just more information, because if the "volenti not fit injura" principle is not in effect, then the employee is in a coercive situation. This problem of coercion must be alleviated before justification on the basis of informed voluntariness can be achieved. Pettit's idea of contestability will then be applied. The firm must satisfy three conditions in order to make effective contestability possible. There must be a basis and channels for contest, which means that there must be transparency as well as effective measures to make grievances heard. There must also be a forum of contest where proper hearings of contestations are guaranteed.

**Keywords**: Contestability, Consent, Ignorance, Incomplete Contracts, Employment Contracts

**JEL codes**: A13, D02, D86, J50

## 1. INTRODUCTION

In this article, my first aim is to show that the standard transaction cost explanation in the economics of the employment contract is in conflict with the standard moral justification of employer authority by consent to such contracts. I take the standard moral position to be that employment contracts, and hence employer authority, gains its justification by the free and voluntary consent of the parties. In economics, I assume that the consensus is that employment contracts are necessarily incomplete. Rather than stating terms for all contingencies, they leave future decisions to the discretion of the employer. This is the rational response of the parties to future unforeseen events. There are alternatives to the moral theory that I discuss and there could be other empirical theories about employment, but my focus is *exclusively* on these theories of consent and incomplete contracts. The core point of the paper is that in their standard interpretations, the ideas of consent and incomplete contracts lead to the conclusion that the acts of authority of the employer cannot have been justified by prior consent.

Employment contracts would seem to be typical examples of "capitalist acts between consenting adults" [Nozick 1974, p. 163]. What could possibly be problematic about them? Agents in the market are thought of as being informed of the consequences of their actions and not coerced; hence, their acts are voluntary. The argument I will make in this paper is, briefly, that if the contemporary economics of the employment contract is correct, then in order to explain the existence of such contracts, we must make the assumption that the contracting parties are attempting to deal with transaction cost caused by ignorance concerning future events. This is the reason why they agree to an incomplete contract in which the employer has authority; in unforeseen situations the employer can decide what should be done. If this ignorance postulate is in effect, the course of action that the employer chooses to take cannot be justified by consent given at the time of the writing of the contract, since the informedness criterion of consent could not have been satisfied due to this ignorance. This is necessarily the case, since the information needed to provide a consent-based justification of such acts is exactly what is lacking, and this lack of information is precisely the reason why rational economic agents would agree to form an incomplete contract, such as the employment contract.

The question, then, is whether employer authority can be justified in some other manner. The second aim of my article is to make plausible – not prove – that in order to achieve justification on the basis of informed and voluntary choice, there must be a real possibility to contest employers' decisions. Providing the lacking information is not sufficient to solve the lack of consent. If employer authority is not justified by prior consent, then it follows that the principle of "*volenti non fit injura*" is not in effect within the employment contract. Therefore, situations where employers act from authority come out as coercive according to the standard view of consent. This problem of coercion must also be alleviated before justification on the basis of informed voluntariness can be achieved. Here, I will adapt the idea of contestability put forward by Philip Pettit and sketch its features and feasibility for the workplace. I attempt this because the ideal of contestability is based on the same values as the standard view of consent, which makes it an attractive approach to try if the standard view fails to achieve justification of employer authority. The firm must satisfy three requisites in order to make effective contestation possible. There must be a *basis* and *channels* for contestation, which means that there must be transparency and effective measures to make grievances heard. There must also be a *forum* for contestation, where proper hearings of contestations are guaranteed. It should be noted that there is another approach that one could take to the question I investigate, which would be to focus on norms in exchange [1]. The primary reason I choose not to pursue that approach here is that I am interested in what appears to be the standard view: the employer has discretion that is justified by consent.

The outline of the paper is as follows. In section two, I will discuss the ideas of voluntariness and informedness that underpin the idea of consent, and present the "*volenti not fit injura*" principle. Decision theory and consent is discussed in the third section. Section four presents the economics of the firm in general, and, in particular, the idea of the employment relation as regulated by an incomplete contract. The fifth section is devoted to making the argument, on the basis of the theory of incomplete contracts, that consent cannot justify acts of employer authority. Section six

1. See Samuel Bowles [2004] or Colin Camerer [2003]. For a more sceptical view of norms in economics, see Hart [2002].

elaborates the idea of contestability and suggests that a suitably modified version of this idea could help solve the problem of justification of employer action. Some institutional implications of justification by the opportunity to contest decisions are presented. The argument is summarized in the concluding section.

## 2. Information, coercion and consent

It is not uncommon to think that what justifies the employment relationship is the consent of the parties, and in this section, I want to outline what I take to be a standard interpretation of consent as a moral ideal with regard to the economic sphere [2]. When I talk about consent in this paper it will be this ideal that I refer to. The account that I focus on is the standard idea of consent in normative thought about economic matters, as it is brought out in the very helpful analysis provided by Fabienne Peter [2004]. However, I will need to make some further additions to that account, in order to be able to fully discuss the relationship between information and consent.

The idea of consent is used, of course, in many different areas, such as medicine, as well as in several different areas of legal and political philosophy [3]. but Milton Friedman captures the essence of the idea of how consent establishes freedom in market relations. He states, "The possibility of coordination through voluntary cooperation rests on the elementary – yet frequently denied – proposition that both parties benefit from it, provided the transaction is bi-laterally *voluntary* and *informed*" [1962, p. 13]. Both conditions are needed to guarantee that the choices that ground consent are the

2. If I can show that on the least demanding, yet plausible, account of what consent demands, there is a conflict between the way employment contracts work and consent, then I would probably be justified in the conclusion that the same incompatibility will be the case when we consider more demanding (more Kantian) accounts of consent. I will not argue for this point.

3. For an overview of the concept of consent, see Joel Feinberg [1986, chap. 20]. For a general overview with some emphasis on medical ethics, see Ruth R. Faden and Tom L. Beauchamp [1986]. For a more specific view see Paul J. Hoehner [2003].

decisions of the specific person under consideration from a consent perspective. If the choice is not voluntary, clearly the decision to consent is not the party's own. We consent to specific things; if the informedness criterion is not fulfilled, then we cannot say that the party chosen to agree to the particular thing under consideration. It has also been suggested that the persons involved should be autonomous or rational as well, but for our present purposes we can leave this and related complications aside [4]. The two conditions of voluntariness and being informed are two necessary and jointly sufficient conditions for justification by consent.

Voluntariness means, in this literature, the absence of coercion. This is also how voluntariness will be understood in this paper; an act, decision, agreement etc. is voluntary when it has been chosen in circumstances where there is no coercion affecting the choice. The contemporary debate on coercion started with Nozick, and his work makes a good starting point for the discussion here as well. One of the first examples in the classic paper "Coercion" [5] concerns the difference between being unfree and being coerced [6]. "You threaten to get me fired from my job if I do A, and I refrain from doing A because of this threat and am coerced into not doing A" [Nozick 1997, p. 16]. Coercion means that a person threatens another with some adverse outcome(s) if that other person chooses some particular act, and both parties know that this is the case [7]. In a robbery, the victim has a choice between

4. We can assume that if the parties are rational enough to participate in the market for work, then they are rational enough. See Feinberg [1986, pp. 113-117] on the unattainable ideal of full voluntariness and the issue of finding what might be considered voluntary enough.

5. Robert Nozick, "Coercion" [1969] is reprinted *in* Robert Nozick [1997].

6. Nozick argues that one is free to, say, walk away from a bluffing robber that claims he has a gun in his trench coat pocket. Hence, being coerced, as in this case, is not sufficient to show that one is unfree. Furthermore, coercion is not a necessary condition for being unfree. You are unfree to rob a bank even though no one coerces you not to do it [1997, pp. 15-16].

7. Nozick [1997, pp. 16-19] presents this list of conditions on coercion:

1) P threatens to bring about or have brought about some consequence if Q does A (and knows he's threatening to do this);

handing over his money or giving up his life, but the robber has significantly changed the payoffs for all other alternatives apart from delivering the money to the robber. If a person changes the payoffs of another person's alternatives for the worse, without that person's consent, the situation is coercive.

Consider this question: Is it a coercive threat or an offer, if a slave-owner says to a slave that he will not be beaten the next day, as he usually is, if he performs some act x? What is the baseline against which we should measure whether the value of an alternative has become worse? If we take the baseline to consist of the expectations of the slave, either subjective or more objective statistical expectations, then this appears to be an offer, regardless of what x is [8]. This seems wrong, and points us in the direction of a moral baseline. The baseline should, in other words, be taken to be a situation where moral rights are respected. The only question concerning the moral baseline for consent that will be discussed in this paper will be Nozick's example of the threat of getting someone fired [9]. Therefore I will refrain from digging deeper into

2) A with this threatened consequence is rendered substantially less eligible as a course of conduct for Q than A without the threatened consequence;

3) P makes this threat in order to get Q not to do A, intending that Q realize he's been threatened by P;

4) Q does not do A;

5) Part of Q's reasons for not doing A is to avoid (or lessen the likelihood of) the consequence which P has threatened to bring about or have brought about;

6) Q knows that P has threatened to do the something mentioned in 1, if he, Q, does A;

7) Q believes that, and P believes that Q believes that, P's threatened consequence would leave Q worse off, having done A, than if Q didn't do and P didn't bring about the consequence.

8. The question comes, and discussion, comes from Nozick [1997, pp. 28-29]. For some, the moral baseline answer seems to pack too much of what is interesting about coercion into the concept of rights. There is another way to answer the baseline questions, the Pareto approach, where contracts that fail the Pareto test in some version, can be held as coercive. See Michael J. Trebilcock [1993, pp. 78-84] for an instructive introduction to the baseline problem and a discussion of the Pareto alternative. My impression is that the literature here is more concerned with what contracts that can be held as void, rather than the question of what defines consent.

9. See Serena Olsaretti [1998] for a forceful critique of the idea of a moral baseline.

this complex issue, and instead assume, with Nozick, that such a threat is a violation of the voluntariness condition.

But then it seems that Friedman's view of the relationship between freedom and capitalism runs into trouble almost before it gets off the ground. Since a capitalist economy consists of firms, it appears that there is ample opportunity for coercion every time an employer exercises his or her right to give orders, and in particular if they fire employees for not following orders. There ought to be a difference between one's employer threatening to have one fired for not doing A and a person on the street doing the same thing [10]. This is where the principle of *volenti non fit injura* makes its entrance. It means that one is not wronged by actions that one has consented to. A rough translation of the Latin would be "if you consent you cannot complain" [Bachman 2003, p. 1033]. Since this principle provides justification for *prima facie* blameworthy acts, it is deeply important that consent has been given under the right conditions. To be wronged is usually understood as suffering the morally relevant kind of harm. As Joel Feinberg puts it: "A person can indeed be harmed by what he consents to, in the sense that his interest may be set back, but he cannot be wronged" [1986, p. 100; cf. Feinberg 1984, pp. 115-117]. Of course, we can say that it is bad to be fired, the idea goes, but it does not constitute harm in the morally relevant way [11]. More precisely, because one has consented to authority in the employment relationship, one has, under voluntary and informed conditions, given permission to the employer to bring about certain outcomes, which without consent would have been immoral [12].

10. Obviously, this requirement is only reasonable for some As. Robbery still is immoral, even if takes place within the bounds of the employment contract.

11. In this context it should be pointed out, as Robert Goodin does [2006], that consent of the parties does not fully justify an agreement if there are third party effects.

12. Obviously, there is a huge debate on whether there are certain things that we cannot consent to, such as prostitution or surrogate parenting, regardless of whether the conditions on consent are satisfied. See Trebilcock [1993] for an overview. The question that I am concerned with in this paper does not turn on what the right answer is in that discussion, and I will not pursue the question of substantial limits on consent in the remainder of the article.

It is the contract, then, that allegedly makes coercion a non-issue within the employment relationship. In order for the employment contract to be justified, it must have been agreed to under non-coercive circumstances. The second condition on consent is that the parties must be informed. In the course of investigating the ideal of fully autonomous choosing, Joel Feinberg spells out two interesting criteria concerning the level of information needed for perfectly free choice[13]:

> – Not because of ignorance (mistake) of factual circumstances
> – Not because of ignorance of the likely consequences of the various alternatives open to him [Feinberg 1986, p. 115, Diagram 20-5].

As Feinberg points out, the ideal of perfectly voluntary and informed choice is unattainable. The question then is what is informed enough? While it is difficult to find precise criteria of how informed the agent should be in the literature, the area of medical ethics provides some guidelines. Tom Beauchamp and James Childress point out that, among other things, medical professionals are obliged to disclose "those facts or descriptions that patients or subjects usually consider material in deciding whether to refuse or consent to the proposed intervention or research" [2001, p. 81]. In general, for consent, there is no implication that some specified agent should provide the information, but there is a demand that the information should be available. As it stands this condition is not directly applicable to the employment contract, but it is easy to see how it could be reformulated in a more general way. I suggest the following general criterion on informedness: *In order for agents to be informed they must have access to those facts or descriptions that such agents usually consider material in deciding whether to refuse or consent to the proposed act.*

13. This is done in the process of trying to spell out a theory of soft paternalism, but it should be noted that the issue of paternalism is distinct from the question of justification by consent. One could well think that employer authority is not justified by consent, while being against paternalistic intervention to remedy this. The alternatives might be worse.

This provides us with a *reasonable person-standard* for the level of information needed for consent. In this the suggested criterion follows Beauchamp and Childress. It does not demand perfect information, but it says that asking what level of information a hypothetical reasonable person would demand sets the level of knowledge needed for consent. There are several ways to make this condition more precise. A high level of knowledge interpretation would say, e.g. that a bus driver must know the exact shade of the colour of the bus she will be driving, whereas a low level interpretation, would say that it is sufficient that she knows that she will be working in the transportation industry. Luckily, for my purpose in this paper, we need not to deliver a fully specified account of the informedness condition. All that is needed for my argument is to point out that Feinberg's conditions put a lower bound on what level of knowledge the agents must have; a reasonable person would demand to know what he or she is consenting to. Since ignorance of factual circumstances means that putatively voluntary consent cannot be justified, we can make two points. First, we need to know what we consent to. We must some have information about the specific issue that is in need of justification. Second, if there is no knowledge to be had, if we act under ignorance, then consent is impossible. When I say that consent is impossible, I do not mean that is impossible for any kind of agreement to take place. I mean that given that the informedness criterion is not satisfied, agreements do not lead to justification in the sense that would put the principle of *volenti non fit injura* in effect.

We shall investigate the issue of information and consent further in the next section, but by the way of concluding this discussion on the value of consent, there are a few further considerations that must be raised. First, the ideal of justification by consent is not a consequentialist idea. We would change our fundamental norm of evaluation, if we said that we should assume that a person has consented when an analysis of costs and benefits show that then the net of benefit of doing so is positive. Such utilitarian reasoning is an alternative to the ideal of consent, not a plausible specification of this deontological ideal. Second, it is important to distinguish the point just made from the view that consent can never be overridden by other considerations. Even if it were true that consent cannot justify commands based on an incomplete contract, one could still hold the view that military personnel ought to always follow the commands of their superiors in battle, if one thinks that any another system would be too dangerous and that it is more important to avoid this danger than to uphold consent.

## 3. Decision theory, information and consent

To investigate further the issue of what information is needed in order for consent to take place, a quote from Richard Posner is useful. He states, "[i]t is my contention that a person who buys a lottery ticket and then loses the lottery has 'consented' to the loss so long as there is no question of fraud or duress" [1981, p. 94]. The idea here is that if a person understands how the lottery works and what the odds are, then he or she also knows that there is a given probability that he or she will gain nothing by entering it. In this context it is useful to consider a standard distinction in decision theory concerning three types of decisions and their relations to knowledge. Choices can be made under certainty, risk or uncertainty [Duncan Luce and Raiffa 1957, pp. 12-15].

In a decision under certainty, the outcomes are fully known, so that you can be certain, for example, that if you choose box A you get candy and if you choose box B you get an electric shock. Consent with this level of information is, obviously, unproblematic. In choices under risk, we have a set of alternatives and known probabilities for each outcome. In this case, we have situations where we are not sure whether we will get an electric shock or candy, but we know that there is, say, a 50/50 chance of either outcome. We can evaluate the outcomes in turn. We can now see how we can consent to lotteries. Taking for granted that we have the correct probability estimates[14], we can say that what is

14. Otherwise we might violate Feinberg's condition about ignorance about likely consequences.

important is that we know what the alternative outcomes are, not that they will be realized with a definite probability. Posner's example is a straightforward decision under risk, and in such situations we know what is relevant, namely the possible alternative outcomes that are available. In this regard, it is hard to argue against the idea that lotteries are consented to, even if one would like to point out that the exercise becomes much more complex. The third type of choice that is usually considered in standard decision theory is choice under uncertainty. For such choices, we lack probability estimates, but there is still a set of alternatives to consider. Even if we do not know the probabilities, we can go through the alternatives in turn, and consent is possible.

These points are based on the idea that it is possible for agents to entertain all possible outcomes. If the set of alternatives becomes too expansive, then this is not feasible. This leads us to a fourth possible type of decision, which is not as frequently discussed [15]. This variety can be called choice or decision under radical uncertainty, but is probably best labeled choice under ignorance [16]. We do not know what the alternative outcomes are in this case. Here, the strategy of going through the alternatives is impossible, either because of the sheer size of the set of outcomes or because the future is indeterminate for some reason. Sven Ove Hansson calls this "decision-making under unknown possibilities" [1996, p. 376]. Can there be consent in such situations? It seems not. In such situations, we do not have information about the future alternatives that might materialize. In Feinberg's terms, there is ignorance of factual circumstances.

The problem is not that we lack full information – to demand that would arguably be utopian – but that there is no information. It is obvious that the information conditions cannot be satisfied, if

15. Perhaps due to Richard C. Jeffery's [1983] way of showing that if our preferences are rational, we can always define a set of alternatives, even under ignorance. Unfortunately, this solution does not help much because if we do not know the particulars of the future we cannot assign proper values to the alternatives under consideration. I thank John Cantwell for pointing this out to me.

16. Here I follow Michael D. Resnik [1987, pp. 13-17].

we do not know the possible outcomes; we would not know what we have consented to. In situations where some outcomes are known, we can consent to those. But unknown possibilities cannot satisfy the information condition, since they are per definition unknown. The only way we could say that there is sufficient information for justification would be to argue that the fact that we have knowledge about other options somehow justifies saying that we have enough information about possibilities that are unknown. That seems unreasonable. Unless we consider agents that are lacking information as being informed enough for the purpose of justification, consent is impossible for choices under ignorance[17]. This conclusion seems welcome given that proper consent would lead *volenti* to come into effect. If you have consented you cannot complain, seems an irrelevant thing to say when previously unknown possibilities materialize. If there is no information at all, this must be in breach of the informedness condition, regardless of how we specify the informedness condition.

## 4. THE INCOMPLETE EMPLOYMENT CONTRACT

In 1962, in *Capitalism and Freedom*, Friedman stated that:

> Despite the important role of enterprises and of money in our actual economy, and despite the numerous and complex problems they raise, the central characteristic of the market technique of achieving co-ordination is fully displayed in the simple exchange economy that contains neither enterprises nor money. [1962, p. 14]

If this were the case, we could see all the essential characteristics of free and voluntary cooperation by investigating how a simple spot market works. There is no relevant difference between

17. Perhaps we could say that consent is only applicable within bounds. One way of explicating this idea would be to turn to David Lewis's [1979] theory of permission. To give permission for Lewis is to assent to a set of possible worlds. This would mean that the bounds of consent are given. However, this would just reformulate the issue under consideration as a question of decision under risk or uncertainty. If we know the set of possible worlds, then we do not face a choice under ignorance.

the market for labor and the fruit market on this account. About the same time that Friedman published his classic book, a new perspective started to emerge on why not all goods are traded in spot markets, which forces us to reconsider whether we can actually disregard firms, or for that matter employment contracts, when thinking about the market – and, as we shall see, consent. The beginnings of an answer to the puzzle of why there are enterprises at all appeared in the writings of Ronald Coase in the thirties, started to gain momentum with the publication of his paper "The Problem of Social Cost" [1960] and has now become mainstream [18]. The answer is that the enterprise is an efficient solution to problems of transaction cost. In this section, I will try to outline the transaction cost approach to the employment contract. This constitutes the second of the two standard views that make up the focus of this paper.

Transaction cost economics attempts to explain the existence of both firms and employment contracts by showing how they are rational responses to transaction costs, and focuses on how parties try to design contracts to handle these costs. Transaction cost economics "deals with how rights to decide, control and coerce are allocated between the parties" [Brousseau and Glachant 2002, p. 15]. The central issue is the "[c]reation of procedures for decision making *ex post* and of mechanisms to render the commitment enforceable" [Brousseau and Glachant 2002, p. 15, table 1.1]. Oliver Williamson explicates the notion of transaction cost as "the comparative costs of planning, adapting, and monitoring task completion under alternative governance structures" [1985, p. 2]. The firm is a private ordering mechanism, an *ex post* institution of contract, for settling disputes and disagreements [*cf.* Williamson 1985, p. 18]. The market is not always used as a governance mechanism, since hierarchical solutions (such as firms or states) are more efficient under some configurations of transaction cost. For a simple exchange of money for fruit, the market is a very efficient

18. For an overview and interpretation of the literature that this paper and Coase's "The Nature of the Firm" [1937] have given rise to with concern to, see Yoram Barzel and Levis A. Kochin [1992].

mechanism, whereas for more complex pursuits such as building cars we may need a more complicated system of cooperation.

Douglas Allen [2000] points out that it is important to keep the two senses of transaction costs apart. In neo-classical economics, the term is used to designate costs associated with meeting at the market, whereas according to the transaction cost view, it is used for all the costs of cooperation. What causes these costs? Allen states: "Regardless of which stream of literature is examined, the underlying theme for transaction costs is the notion of ignorance" [2000, p. 906] Ignorance plays an essential explanatory role in the economics of contract. Information cost, caused by ignorance, is a necessary condition for transaction cost, but it is not sufficient; there must also be cooperation. For example, Robinson Crusoe had information costs to deal with before Friday showed up, but it was not until they met that there were any transaction costs. When there is a lack of information and a need for cooperation, there is transaction cost.

To return to the car-building example, when cooperating to manufacture cars, we must try to take into account future changes in demand, technology, taste, climate, business cycles as well as the possibility of other unpredicted events. The rational course of action will depend on these contingencies, which will for the most part be unforeseen. This in turns means that what course of action that will have to be pursued will also be unforeseen. This kind of ignorance accounts for an essential difference between exchanges on spot markets and the focus of rest of this section: employment contracts.

When parties meet to come to an employment agreement they face transaction costs in at least two important forms: first, costs caused by the impossibility of foreseeing all relevant future events and forming proper responses to these; and, second, costs that come from the prohibitive cost of actually negotiating such a complete contract, even if all future states of the world were possible to foresee [Milgrom and Roberts 1992, p. 330] [19]. There are two

19. Actually, the authors also talk of a third form of ignorance, concerning the problem of unambiguously describing future events and responses in a way that makes a

general reasons why parties remain ignorant about the future in the contract situation; either it is too costly to predict, or it is, for epistemic reasons, difficult or impossible. In the first case, it would be irrational to try to figure out future events. The second kind of uncertainty is of a deeper sort. The shape of the decision tree (or parts of it) is necessarily unknown. This situation is either due to the future being indeterminate or due to the cognitive limitations (bounded rationality) of the parties making the decisions such that they are unable to predict the future. In both cases, knowledge of the future is constrained. What should be done?

> Uncertainty about the conditions that will prevail when a contract is being executed together with complexity of the task make it impossible, or at least uneconomical, to determine in advance what should be done in every possible contingency, so the contract that is written will generally be less determinate than in a simpler setting. [Milgrom and Roberts 1992, p. 32]

The parties solve, or rather try to get around, the problem of transaction costs by agreeing on an *incomplete contract.* The employment contract is such a contract, as "it does not specify each party's obligations in every conceivable eventuality" [Vandenberghe 2000, p. 552]. For instance, no auto industry worker has it written into his or her contract what is demanded of him or her if financial disaster hits at the same time as consumer tastes change and new environmental regulations are put in place. The potential for such complex changes in the environment indicate that the set of possible outcomes will be too large for the parties to get an overview of in the initial contract situation. The employment contract is also a *relational contract.* Such contracts "serve to structure the relationship and set common expectations, and they establish mechanisms that will be used to make decisions and allocate costs and benefits" [Milgrom and Roberts 1992, p. 132]. This means that in the car-manufacturing firm, manage-

contract enforceable in court. This is the problem of indescribable contingencies. I am not sure that this problem does not reduce to one of the other sources of ignorance, and I will focus on them in what follows.

ment will have to decide how to allocate labor and other resources. A relational contract is often supported by an implicit contract. Such a contract is, hopefully, a shared view on the relationship; however, it is not legally binding[20]. The parties can consider these norms or principles binding on each other's behavior, but they are unenforceable.

A key issue to settle is which party to the contract will have the authority to decide what to do when contingencies occur. This is important because that agent's interpretation of the norms will stand and other interpretations will be unenforceable. Instead of explicit conditions stated in a contract, we have an authority that deals with the unforeseen. The employment contract is relational in this sense; when contingencies occur, one party (the employer) gets to decide. This is, then, what provides the economic motivation for authority in the firm. Milgrom and Roberts state the issue of employer authority straightforwardly: "The decision mechanism in the employment contract is basically that the boss can order the employee to do anything that is not explicitly forbidden by the contract's terms or by law" [1992, p. 330].

The core idea is, then, that there must be someone in charge when we cannot predict the future. Why should this always be the same party? The usual explanation is that, firstly, it is more efficient to have one party decide than to bargain relentlessly and, secondly; it is more efficient to have the same party decide than to alternate. There are two accounts in the literature as to why the party that should have authority is the owner of physical capital. The first is that he or she bears a greater risk than the owners of human capital do in the relationship and the second account is based on the idea that he or she has a deeper interest in the reputation of the firm [Milgrom and Roberts 1992, pp. 330-332].

This leaves the question of how authority is to be understood. If we can leave jobs, in what sense could this be called authority? Why are commands at work not like suggestions, but instead expressions of authority? Part of the answer is that if you are fired,

20. See for instance Vandenberghe [2000, p. 549]. For a discussion on the difficulties of adjudicating implied terms in contracts, see also George M. Cohen [2000].

or if you quit by your own choice, you will be subject to cost from, for instance, losing your firm-specific human capital and being subject to the transaction cost involved in finding a new job. This is something that every auto industry worker in present circumstances knows. A second part of the answer has to do with the so-called efficiency wage theory of the employment relationship, which says that it is possible to achieve Pareto improvements through the employer paying a rent to the employee in exchange for extra effort, under the threat of not renewing the relationship [Milgrom and Roberts 1992, pp. 250-261] [21]. There are, hence, costs (lost rents) that ensue from not following directives from authority within the firm, regardless of if you quit or if you are fired. These costs would be easily avoidable if a spot market properly modelled the employment relationship. As we have seen, it does not [*cf.* Hseih 2005].

## 5. Consent and incomplete contracts

Let us now bring together what I have referred to as the two standard views. The first standard view is that employer authority is morally justified by informed and voluntary consent to the employment contract. The second standard view says that in order to explain why rational individuals on a market would agree to incomplete contracts, such as the employment contract, it is necessary to assume that the parties to the contract are facing a decision under ignorance. Now the first aim of this paper is, as I have said, to show that the standard transaction cost explanation of the employment contract is in conflict with the standard moral justification of employer authority by consent to such contracts. The problem that I want to bring out can be seen when we find that starting from these two standard views we can conclude the following: Employer authority is explained by ignorance and justified by consent.

21. For another version of such an argument, see Samuel Bowles [2004, chap. 8].

However, we have also seen that consent under ignorance is impossible, since the information condition cannot be satisfied. At the same time, economic agents would only opt for incomplete contracts and employer authority when there is ignorance. This brings us to my main point: it seems impossible to consent to *acts* of authority that are based on an incomplete contract. The relevant information about *these acts* will be missing, because for every case where there is a need for authority due to ignorance about the future, the situation where this need occurs has not been predicted. If it had been predicted, a method to resolve the situation could have been put in the contract, and thus the situation could have been handled without authority. Consent does not lead to justification if it is due to ignorance of factual circumstances. If the situation could not have been predicted, then it could not have been properly consented to, because the information clause for consent would not have been satisfied. It is exactly the unknown possibilities that explain why there are employment contracts that also show that the information condition cannot have been satisfied. Information about the contingency is not available to the parties *ex ante*. If consent demands some level of information higher than zero, then no act of authority based on incomplete contracts can be regarded as justified by consent.

Note that even if one or both of the standard accounts are mistaken, *i.e.* if consent is not an appropriate ideal of justification or if there is a better empirical explanation of employment contracts, the point that these two accounts come into conflict still stands. Anyone who is committed to both of these two positions will have to face the conflict between informedness and ignorance.

But that the argument does not, however, imply that one cannot justifiably enter into employment contracts on the basis of consent. It seems clear that the agents can have access to those facts or descriptions of acts that they usually consider material when deciding whether to agree to such contracts. Recall that we said above that the information must be about the right things. The parties can be informed about policies, values and personnel, when considering entering the employment relationship. This is, I assume, information enough to consider the relationship of authority inherent in employment justified by informed consent. The employee can even agree to the idea that the employer gets to choose what polices should be implemented when contingencies occur. This would create a presumption in favour of the policy that the decisions of the employer should be carried out. However, when the employer takes these decisions, we find ourselves in situations that were unforeseen at the signing of the contract. Therefore, the content of these decisions are not justified by consent. To sum up, the entering *into* employment contracts can be justified by consent, but within this relationship acts of authority cannot be justified by that prior consent. The relationship between the employer and employee can be justified by consent, but not the content of the decisions that the employer takes.

As we saw above, the literature has identified two different causes of ignorance. In both cases, the material facts in our criterion of informedness are missing. This is obvious in the case where it is epistemologically impossible for the parties to predict the future. However, it might be objected that in situations where ignorance is due only to the costliness of information, and the condition on voluntariness is satisfied, the problem of consent could have been avoided if the parties had spent the required resources to find out what would happen. Therefore, one might say that the lack of consent is not particularly problematic; we have come close enough to proper justifying consent. There is much to be said for letting costs play a role in deciding how to specify the information condition, but the lower limit on any such specification is the demand that consent is not based on ignorance. Furthermore, saying that we are close enough to proper consent is problematic, since it would imply that an act by one person A towards another person B is justified by such alleged consent if it would have been possible for B, through some use of resources, to have predicted this act. However, this would amount to giving up consent since justification would then loose its connection to actual agreements between the parties. It would mean that B could be considered as having given consent to an act that he or she actually has never considered, nor *a fortiori* agreed to, which would seem a clear-cut violation of the demands of the *volenti* principle.

In terms of protection of personal integrity, it would also be peculiar to say that in order to be protected, you must act irrationally. Remember that *ex hypotesi* the cost of writing a complete contract would be so high that it would be irrational not to settle for incompleteness. The cause of ignorance is irrelevant when we investigate whether proper consent has been given or not.

The problem of consent in situations where information is lacking might not seem very difficult to solve; we could simply provide the required information. However, an implication of the claim that the informedness condition is not satisfied is that *volenti non fit injura* cannot be in effect when it comes to acts of employer authority. Therefore, we are lead to a second claim: the employee is in a coercive situation within the employment relationship. Remember that in order for *volenti* to provide moral justification for putatively coercive actions, these actions must have had been properly consented to, but since the informedness condition is not fulfilled, proper consent cannot have not been given. If *volenti* does not apply, then management directives are coercive. Returning to Nozick's example: the important difference, from the perspective of the standard view of consent, between the man on the street threatening to get a person fired from his job and his employer issuing a warning that he may be dismissed, is that in the latter case *volenti* is in effect. When this principle is not satisfied, the same baseline, with regard to what should count as coercive, ought to be in effect after the signing of the employment contract as prior to the agreement between the employer and the employee. More information never solves a problem of coercion; we must look elsewhere for that.

Does what I am saying imply also that it is impossible to consent to an operation if one cannot foresee every medical decision that the physician will have to perform? If consent under ignorance is impossible, it seems that one cannot consent to having an operation if one does not know what measures the physician will take. Here it is important to note that the argument that I have proposed does not question that one can consent to being in a specific relationship to an employer, or a doctor. The point I have stressed concerns the justification for the actions that the employer or doctor later chooses. In medicine, a basic function of consent is to protect the weaker party against the more powerful party. The physician decides how to perform the operation, and this authority is constrained by strict rules on informed consent. During medical treatment, the patient can always withdraw his consent, and new consent must be sought if the treatment is changed. The doctor cannot, obviously, threaten the patient with consequences if he or she does not choose to do what the doctor suggests.

In the workplace, the employee does not have authority, and in this sense, he is, like the patient, the weaker party. Moreover, if a patient has given her consent to being treated by a physician, this would *not* make it at all reasonable to invoke *volenti*, in the case that the patient is displeased with the treatment offered by the physician. Rather, in medicine we would want to take every feasible measure to see to it that it would be as easy and painless as possible for the patient to change his mind. Obviously, in the workplace we have other goals than in the hospital and we strive for other things then full autonomy, but the point here is about justification, not goals or preferences for autonomy. The analogy does not show, I claim, that the demands I have made on the justification of employer authority are too stringent. Instead, it shows that in potentially coercive situations, we do not think that prior consent is enough. The medical example is not a *reductio*, but an illustration.

However, this is not a perfect analogy. The strategies used in medicine would not fit very well in the context of the workplace because it would externalize the costs of consent on other employees. In medicine, we face individual choices, but when it comes to employment we have entered a social context, rather than the individual context where consent is usually considered; we are *within* the employment relationship. For instance, it would be impossible to run firms if every management directive would have to be consented to in advance. Furthermore, if we insisted on prior consent, we would be forced to give up on any moral justification of the kind of incomplete and relational contracts that employment contracts are examples of. We could take all this to mean that employment is inherently coercive and that that no kind of employer authority could ever be justified. Of course, if we in some way ban employer authority, then consent will justify what is left of the workplace relationships. But before we come to this radical conclusion, we should investigate if there exists a method of justification that respects the consent to the employment relationship and that includes a presumption in favour of the decisions that the employer takes, while based on free and voluntary choice in a way that does not cause too heavy externalities on the other members of the firm. We should be looking for a method of justification appropriate for use within the social context of the employment relationship.

We might then be tempted to take a hint from Richard Posner who is ready to accept less than proper consent, when it cannot be obtained: "If there is no reliable mechanism for eliciting express consent, it follows not that we must abandon the principle of consent but that we should be satisfied with implied (or more precisely, perhaps, hypothetical) consent where it exists" [1981, p. 96]. To be satisfied with hypothetical consent, however, might have some unfortunate consequences. In political philosophy, this idea has been taken to mean that as long as people do not emigrate they have hypothetically consented to the government of the country wherein they are residing[22]. It would allow us to say that whatever happens within the firm has been consented to, and thus is justified, as long as it does not lead the employee to quit, (and, of course, as long as it is not illegal). The problem with the idea that employer actions can be justified in this way is that if we have agreed that prior consent does not justify acts of authority, then such authority is still unjustified even with the exit option in place. The reason that we can even talk about employer authority is that it is costly for the employee not to follow the directives of the management. If the employee quits, she has been punished twice,

22. It should be noted that the idea of consent, be it explicit or implicit, plays many different roles in political philosophy. In the discussion above it fills an important part for some theories of political obligation, but there are also consent theories on subjects such as the nature of justice and the justification of the state.

first by being the object of an unjustified employer demand and then by having to bare the costs of this directive by quitting. It is therefore hard to see how merely hypothetical consent would help with the issue of moral justification. If the employee does not quit, then we have no reason in advance to assume that this is because she agrees with the directive. It might equally well have to do with the cost of quitting. Clearly, just like in political philosophy, this justifies too much.

But there is something to this intuition. It needs proper background institutions in order to provide justification. We can find a way of justifying acts of authority (even if this authority will be more constrained than the kind we started out investigating) by voluntary and informed choice suitable for the employment context if we turn to the political philosophy of Philip Pettit and his attempt to solve the problem of restricting arbitrary political authority.

## 6. Contestability at work

Now, if we began as convinced about the usefulness of the standard theory of justification by consent, but was then persuaded that it does not work for acts of authority, we would wonder where to turn instead. My suggestion is that we appropriate the concept of contestability from Pettit's theory of republicanism [1997, 2001, 2000]. My aims in this section are modest and two-fold. I want to sketch the implications of the idea of contestability for the workplace, and indicate how that ideal could justify some recognizable institutional features that we can see in actual work-places around the world. I will also attempt to show that values of voluntariness and informedness are incorporated in the theory of contestability, in a way that should be attractive to the proponents of the standard theory of consent. To be clear, I do not aim to solve the problem of how consent can justify employer authority – if my argument above is correct, there is no such solution – but instead I will attempt to show that there is an alternative, but related, method of justification that will work and that should appeal to proponents of the standard consent view.

According to this Pettit's political philosophy, freedom, understood as non-domination, should be maximized. The ideal of non-domination says that freedom is achieved when no one has the capacity to interfere on an arbitrary basis with one's actions. Republicanism focuses on how to secure such freedom, and here Pettit argues that consent is not sufficient since any system of law will leave discretion in the hands of public officials. He says that:

> Whether a relationship sprang originally from a contract or not, whether or not it was consensual in origin, the fact that it gives one party the effective capacity to interfere more or less arbitrarily in some other's choices means that one person dominates or subjugates the other. [1997, p. 62]

Therefore, Pettit suggests that non-domination has more to do with the possibility to contest actions. In this vein, Pettit has argued that we should conceive of democracy as having two dimensions, an authorial and an editorial aspect.

> What democratic institutions have to do is, first, to establish an authorial dimension of control – control by ordinary people – for searching out and generating a rich supply of presumptive common-interest policies; and second to establish an editorial dimension of control – again, control by ordinary people – for rigorously scrutinizing and eliminating those candidate policies and those modes of policy implementation that do not advance common, recognizable interests. [2000, p. 116]

The first dimension is handled by the basic democratic mechanisms, such as freedom of expression and open elections. The second dimension concerns the possibility to contest acts and decisions. This means that the justification of public actions comes not primarily from consent, but from "their meeting [...] the condition of being such that if they conflict with the perceived interests and ideas of the citizens, then the citizens can effectively contest them" [1997, p. 185]. Pettit says further that, "what matters is not the historical origin of decisions in some form of consent but their modal or counterfactual responsiveness to the possibility of contestation" [1997, p. 185].

We can make use of many insights from this theory without necessarily buying into the full republican theory of freedom. The argument that follows does not really on the republican account on freedom, but only on the mechanism that Pettit presents as a method of securing his favored account of liberty. The idea is that if there is a method of justification that relies on agents being *informed* and acting *voluntarily* and that handles problems that appear systematically with the lack of consent[23], then this method would be a plausible candidate to be tried as a measure to achieve justification within the employment contract.

Let us start with the authorial dimension, which, I believe, can be handled briefly. The ideal of contestability does not demand a specific set of institutions, such as those of a democratic state, and there is, moreover, a set of institutions in the labor market that can fill the authorial roles elections and freedom of speech. A well functioning labor market can serve as a background to choices to entering the employment relationship, similarly to how freedom of expression functions as a background to democratic elections. If the labor market functions well there be a rich supply of different "policies" to choose from. Clearly, the worse this market function, the more difficult will it be for prospective employees to exercise control over the terms of contract and hence determine the terms of cooperation. This may imply that it is a demand of liberty that unemployment is kept low. How then do employees vote? A simple answer would be that they vote by choosing what employment contract to enter. This is how they decide on what "policies" they want to see implemented. We could then say that the authorial aspect is achieved by the employment contract. There

23. For complete contracts that have properly been consented to there seem to be only one way in which acts may be arbitrary; they are breaches of contract. When it comes to incomplete contracts, a further variant appears. An act from authority can also be arbitrary, because it has not been consented to. It seems, then, that here we have a contract that might have sprung from consent but still allows arbitrary actions. The arbitrary power that republicans are concerned with co-varies systematically with the lack of consent.

are explicit terms, even in incomplete contract, and these provide the bounds on the employment relationship. These terms are justified by consent. This is a way of stating the point we have made above; consent can justify the entry into employment contracts.

It is authority that cannot be justified by consent, not complete terms in contracts. The question then is: what is needed for editorial control, proper contestability, to be in place? According to Pettit, the basic preconditions for contestability are, that there is a potential *basis* for contestation, an opportunity for voice, or as I shall say *channels*, and that there is a *forum*. How then could we say that a basis for contestation rules out arbitrariness and leads to informed choice? It does this through providing a standard of cooperation within the contract and by providing the material needed (*i.e.* information) to be able to contest decisions. For a basis of contestability to be operative, some institutional mechanisms must be in place. These mechanisms are consequences of the following requirement for how authorities are to approach every decision. They are to "decide on the basis of suitable considerations and to make clear which considerations are moving them" [Pettit 1997, p. 188]. For every site where decisions are made, there should be procedures that enable citizens to identify the reason for a given decision and to question it. Basically, this means that there should be transparency. The first demand that contestability makes on the workplace is that employees have a right to information that concerns them. Clearly countervailing *prima facie* efficiency arguments could be brought forth here, such as the importance of business secrets and patents, but the starting point should be that the nexus of contracts [24] that is the firm should be transparent to the parties. Transparency remedies the lack of information, and insures that the condition on informedness can be satisfied, but as I have pointed out this does not solve the problem of coercion. We must now turn to methods to insure influence over acts of authority.

24. In the economics literature, this is a standard description of organizations and firms. See, e.g. Milgrom and Roberts [1992, p. 20].

Employees must be able to voice their concerns; there must be channels through which one can contest. This requires, in the political case, "that for any way in which public decision-making may offend against someone's interests or ideas, there are means whereby those interests or ideas can be asserted in response" [Pettit 1997, p. 190]. There must, in the same vein, be actual mechanisms for the employee to voice his or her complaints. This suggests that the rights to appeal and association should be implemented. It also seems to imply that such avenues as ombudsmen, employee hotlines and unions should be in place. In order to have effective voice, the fear of retaliation must be minimized. This can be achieved, to some extent, by formal organizational measures, but might also require a change in how we look at the employment relationship.

Just being able to voice one's complaint does not guarantee that one can influence acts of authority. How can we guarantee that the forum is responsive to contestations? The basic ideas here are that a proper hearing should be guaranteed and that decisions taken with regard to how to handle contestations must also be fair. Procedures should be set up so that authorities cannot "ignore certain challenges that are raised against them. Such bodies should be required to answer for how they behave" [Pettit 1997, pp. 195-196]. The idea of a forum brings to mind a parliament, but as Pettit points out, there may be other forms that are more suitable, depending on empirical circumstances and the purpose of an organization. The German model of co-determination, whereby representatives of the employees take place on the boards of companies, suggests itself as a possible way to implement the notion of a forum in the workplace. A proper hearing is a fair hearing, which indicates that we need a view of fairness within the firm. One way of clearly delineating the idea of fair cooperation in the firm would be to take a Rawlsian approach to the issue and investigate how free and equal co-workers, understood in the vein of Rawls's free and equal citizens, would cooperate [25]. Another approach would be

25. Such a view is outlined *in* Lars Lindblom [2009].

to try to develop a conception of fairness on the basis of the norms that underlies our everyday expectations with regards to employment. There are, of course, many approaches that could be investigated.

Can the ideal of contestability handle our problem with the *volenti* principle not being satisfied and thus Nozick's example of coercion by having someone fired? No and yes. No, since there are only two solutions to the problem of consent that I have identified, and both seem very unattractive: giving up on employment contracts or giving up on consent. The contestability idea is, then, not exactly a solution to our problem, but a sensible substitute for consent where it cannot be had. It allows for justified consent to employment contracts, and guarantees that that any decisions within this relationship are taken in a fair and un-coercive manner. Employers are forced to answer for how they behave by informed employees. In the process of securing the institutional preconditions for fairness, it sees to it that the employee can participate in an un-coerced and informed manner in the evaluation of these decisions. In a social context, it does not seem coercive to have one's case decided by a fair process. We can, then, say that contestability handles the Nozick example, since the idea of contestability seems to be an appropriate method of justification within the employment relationship.

To sum up this brief sketch, what is needed for contestability is transparency with regard to decision-making, channels through which all members of the firm can make their concerns heard in an equitable manner, such as ombudsmen and unions, and a private ordering mechanism that is responsive to contestations and settles them fairly, perhaps in terms of an ideal co-determination process. Ideally, most acts of authority will be justified by not being contested. This is the fundamental hope of the theory of contestability that Pettit speaks of when he points out the importance of counterfactual responsiveness to contestation. This is also one reason why the system of contestability will not greatly hamper decision-making ability, as well as a way of capturing the intuition behind the idea that hypothetical consent justifies employer authority. Further reasons for believing that contestability would not slow down decision-making would be that implementing the contestability ideal involves putting in place mechanisms for coming to agreements and incentives for taking decisions that would not be contested. Furthermore, over time there will develop a body of "case law", which should serve to both lower the rate of new contestations and speed up the handling of them. Contestability is a mechanism based on informed and non-coerced choice that is suitable for the social context. If the employee then wins a contestation in the forum, she has, in an informed manner and without being subject to coercion, exercised her will in a way parallel to what one does when one gives consent to an agreement. If she loses, she has lost on fair terms.

## 7. Conclusion

In this article, I have investigated two standard ideas concerning employment contracts; together they suggest that employer authority is justified by consent, yet explained by ignorance. I have argued that if employment contracts are incomplete for the reason put forward by transaction cost economics, then consent cannot justify acts of authority within the firm. If they are not so justified, then the *volenti* principle is not in effect. Furthermore, if it is not, then employees are in a coercive situation and providing the earlier lacking information will not give justification. I have suggested that if consent is an unfeasible method of justification in the social context, then we should look for some other way of bringing about justification based on informed and un-coerced choice. The idea of contestability can solve the problem of lack of information and alleviate the problem of coercion in the firm in manner suitable for the social context and is based on voluntary and informed choice. If there is a basis for contestation, suitable channels and a forum where contestations are fairly heard within the firm, then acts of authority are justified either if they are not contested or if they are found reasonable in the forum. Executive power remains with the employer, but is conscribed by the power of both employees and employers to contest decisions. On the one hand, there is the employment contract, which leads up to the *prima facie* authority of the employer, but that is justified by the consent of the parties. On the other hand, there is the possibility of contestation, which gives all parties a fair share of the editorial control over the agenda of the workplace.

## REFERENCES

ALLEN D.W., 2000, "Transaction Costs", *in* B. Bouckaert and G. De Geest (eds.), *Encyclopedia of Law and Economics*, vol. I, *The History and Methodology of Law and Economics*, Cheltenham, Edward Elgar, pp. 893-926.

BACHMAN G., 1993, "Volenti Non Fit Iniura: How to Make a Principle Work", *German Law Journal*, 4(10), pp. 1033-1042.

BARZEL Y. and KOCHIN L.A., 1992, "Ronald Coase on the Nature of Social Cost as a Key to the Problem of the Firm", *The Scandinavian Journal of Economics*, 94(1), pp. 19-31.

BEAUCHAMP T.L. and CHILDRESS J.F., 2001, *Principles of Biomedical Ethics*, 5 e ed., Oxford, Oxford UP.

BOWLES S., 2004, *Microeconomics: Behavior, Institutions, and Evolution*, Princeton, Princeton UP.

BROUSSEAU E. and GLACHANT J.-M., 2002, "The Economics of Contract and the Renewal of Economics", in *The Economics of Contracts*, Cambridge, Cambridge UP, pp. 3-30.

CAMERER C., 2003, *Behavioral Game Theory: Experiments in Strategic Interaction*, Princeton, Princeton UP.

COASE R., 1937, "The Nature of the Firm", *Economica*, 4(16), pp. 386-405.

–, 1960, "The Problem of Social Cost", *Journal of Law and Economics*, 3(1), pp. 1-44.

COHEN G.M., 2000, "Implied Terms and Interpretation in Contract Law", *in* B. Bouckaert and G. De Geest (eds.), *Encyclopedia of Law and Economics*, vol. III, *The Regulation of Contracts*, Cheltenham, Edward Elgar, pp. 78-99.

FADEN R.R. and BEAUCHAMP T.L., 1986, *A History and Theory of Informed Consent*, New York, Oxford UP.

FEINBERG J., 1984, *Harm to Others*, New York, Oxford UP.

–, 1986, *Harm to Self*, Oxford, Oxford UP.

FRIEDMAN M., 1962, *Capitalism and Freedom*, Chicago, Chicago UP.

GOODIN R., 2006, "Volenti Goes to Market", *The Journal of Ethics*, 10(1), pp. 53-74.

HANSSON S.O., 1996, "Decision-Making under Great Uncertainty", *Philosophy of the Social Sciences*, 26(3), pp. 369-386.

HART O., 2002, "Norms and the Theory of the Firm", *in* E. Brousseau and J.-M. Glachant (eds.), *The Economics of Contract*, Cambridge, Cambridge UP, pp. 180-191.

HOEHNER P.J., 2003, "Ethical Aspects of Informed Consent in Obstetric Anesthesia", *Journal of Clinical Anesthesia*, 15(8), pp. 587-600.

HSEIH N.-H., 2005, "Rawlsian Justice and Corporate Governance: A Case for Workplace Republicanism", *Social Theory and Practice*, 31(1), pp. 115-143.

JEFFERY R.C., 1983, *The Logic of Decision*, 2e ed., Chicago, University of Chicago Press.

LEWIS D., 1979, "A Problem about Permission", *in* E. Saarinen, R. Hilpinen, I. Niiniluoto and M.B. Hintikka (eds.), *Essays in Honour of Jaakko Hintikka*, Dordrecht, Reidel, pp. 163-175.

LINDBLOM L., 2009, *The Employment Contract between Ethics and Economics*, PhD diss. Royal Institute of Technology, Stockholm.

LUCE R.D. and RAIFFA H., 1957, *Games and Decisions*, New York, Wiley.

MILGROM P. and ROBERTS J., 1992, *Economics, Organization and Management*, Upper Saddle River, Prentice Hall.

NOZICK R., 1974, *Anarchy, State, and Utopia*, New York, Basic Books.

–, 1997, *Socratic Puzzles*, Cambridge, Harvard UP.

OLSARETTI S., 1998, "Freedom, Force and Choice: Against the Rights-Based Definition of Voluntariness", *Journal of Political Philosophy*, 6(1), pp. 53-78.

PETER F., 2004, "Choice, Consent, and the Legitimacy of Market Transactions", *Economics and Philosophy*, 20(1), pp. 1-18.

PETTIT Ph., 1997, *Republicanism: A Theory of Freedom and Government*, Oxford, Oxford UP.

–, 2000, "Democracy, Electoral and Contestatory", *Nomos*, 42, pp. 105-144.

–, 2001, *A Theory of Freedom*, Cambridge, Polity Press.

POSNER R.A., 1981, *The Economics of Justice*, Cambridge, Harvard UP.

RESNIK M.D., 1987, *Choices*, Minneapolis, University of Minneapolis Press.

TREBILCOCK M.J., 1993, *The Limits of Freedom of Contract*, Cambridge, Harvard UP.

VANDENBERGHE A.-S., 2000, "Labor Contracts", *in* B. Bouckaert and G. De Geest (eds.), *Encyclopedia of Law and Economics*, vol. III, *The Regulation of Contracts*, Cheltenham, Edward Elgar, pp. 541-560.

WILLIAMSON O.E., 1985, *The Economic Institutions of Capitalism*, New York, Free Press.

# LONG-TERM DEVELOPMENTS IN HUMAN LABOR AND THEIR POLITICAL IMPLICATIONS

CHRISTIAN CORDES *

**Résumé**

Cet article propose une analyse des changements qualitatifs dans le travail humain en relation avec l'évolution des fondements épistémiques de la technologie. Le rôle des capabilités humaines dans le développement économique de long terme est décrit et une taxinomie des *inputs* de travail humain est suggérée. Un modèle historique récurrent est identifié : les êtres humains apprennent à transférer avec succès certaines qualités du travail aux machines. Ce qui entraîne ensuite une évolution des exigences adressées au facteur travail ; cela se reflète dans les « capabilités » employées dans les processus de production. Cette approche rend compte des analyses contradictoires de l'organisation du travail proposées dans différents courants de pensée sur l'évolution des compétences. En outre, on démontre que ces processus d'évolution des compétences individuelles peuvent favoriser le développement économique. Des implications politiques sont ensuite discutées.

**Mots-clés** : compétences, changement technologique, changements qualitatifs, marché du travail, politiques (mise en œuvre)

**Abstract**

This paper provides an analysis of the qualitative changes in human labor which are in mutual dependence with the evolution of the epistemic base of technology. The role of human capabilities in long-term economic development is depicted and a

* Max Planck Institute of Economics, Kahlaische Str. 10, 07745 Jena, Germany, cordes@econ.mpg.de.

taxonomy of human labor inputs is suggested. A recurrent historical pattern is identified: humans learned to successively transfer certain qualities of labor to machines. Subsequently, the requirements on labor changed, which is reflected in the complementary qualitative structure of capabilities employed in production. This approach accounts for contradictory patterns in work organization found by different strands of thinking about skill change in technological advancement. Furthermore, it is shown that these processes can trigger self-reinforcing economic developments. Some political implications are discussed.
**Keywords**: Skills, Technological Change, Qualitative Change, Labor Market, Policy Making

**JEL codes**: J21, J24, N30, O33, E60

## 1. Introduction

This paper starts from the observation that the evolving epistemic base of technology significantly affects the qualitative structure of human labor employed in production and *vice versa*[1]. For millions of years humankind has created artifacts that are designed to serve a human purpose and have become essential as an ongoing basis for human life. Therefore, we examine the historical record of long-term qualitative economic change in human labor and suggest some inductive generalizations and taxonomies. Most macro models used by labor economists, human capital theory, and growth theory do not consider the heterogeneity of human input efforts [e.g. Becker 1993; Grossman and Helpman 1991; Hamermesh 1996; Romer 1986]. The concept brought forward here differentiates between different qualities of human skills employed in production and identifies some recurrent patterns in the long-term evolution of labor and technology. For this purpose, a taxonomy of human labor inputs is provided that guides the analysis of the historical material.

1. The term "epistemic base of technology" has been introduced by Mokyr [Mokyr, 2002].

As regards the political implications of these developments, the paper identifies some areas in which economic policy making is called upon. It is shown how the continuous accumulation of production knowledge gives rise to new policy problems and political desiderata. Furthermore, the role of human cognitive labor inputs as constraints to the ongoing knowledge growth process is addressed. Other aspects relate to the changing role of the family in providing certain sorts of labor and employment effects of the continuous qualitative change in the realm of work.

The paper is organized as follows: section two presents historical material to expose the changing role of various sorts of human capabilities as labor inputs in long-term economic development and their interplay with the development of the epistemic base of technology. This section also suggests a systematic way how to bring together the qualities of labor in an unifying taxonomy. Section three identifies some recurrent patterns in long-run economic development and presents some conceptual thoughts that help their understanding. Next, section four focuses on some political implications. The last section concludes.

## 2. THE CHANGING COMPOSITION OF HUMAN SKILLS IN PRODUCTION

Center stage in our analysis are the capabilities humans bring to the production process. A taxonomy of the different human capabilities that became input factors in the course of history is conducive to an analysis of the variety of motives and cognitions underlying heterogeneous labor supply and fundamental driving forces of economic evolution. On this basis, generalizations across events can be made and recurrent patterns in economic evolution can be identified. Figure 1 shows such a taxonomy of human labor inputs.

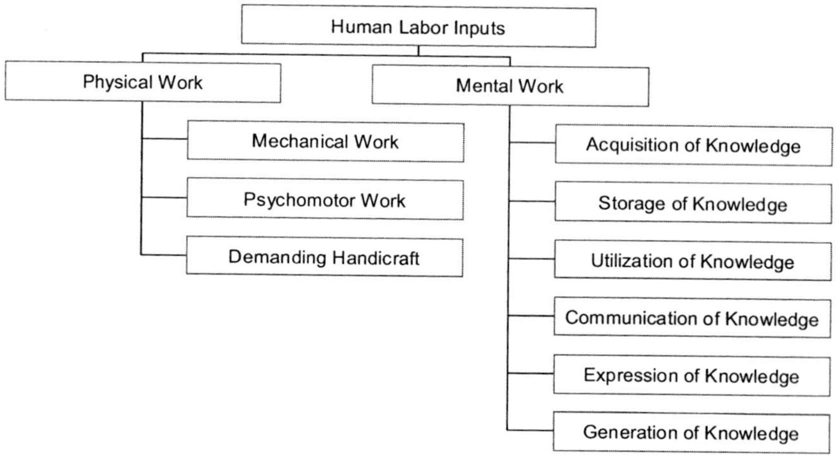


Figure 1
A taxonomy of human labor inputs

The elementary dividing up of human labor encompasses the taxa "physical work" and "mental work". The first category of physical work, "mechanical work", includes physical high-energy-expenditure tasks eventually involving simple tools [Fleishman and Reilly 1992]. The class "psychomotor skills" comprises the coordination of motor functions, such as multilimb coordination, wrist-finger speed, and sensory abilities. The share of repetitive low-energy-expenditure elements is high, while the amount of information to be processed is low. The last aspect of physical labor is that of demanding handicraft. With an extensive amount of manual dexterity, this is the ability to make skillfully coordinated movements of a hand, or of a hand together with its arm, in grasping and manipulating objects.

The taxon "acquisition of knowledge", as the first in the category "mental work", includes manifold learning processes and the utilization of learning opportunities, which are provided by different institutions or persons, such as instruction by parents or collaborators, schooling, higher education, learning-by-doing, imitation, and so on. In the next category, "storage of knowledge", the psychological processes of remembering and memorizing of knowledge are emphasized most. The capability to apply abstractions in specific and concrete task situations belongs to the class "utilization of knowledge". General ideas, rules of procedures, technical principles, and frugal theories are facets of these abstractions [Bloom 1969]. The category "communication of knowledge" comprises the active dissemination of knowledge, for example, via instructive teaching. The taxon "expression of knowledge" refers to the process of turning existing knowledge into tools, machinery, or services. Tasks in this category include the putting together of elements and parts so as to form a whole but nothing genuinely new. Finally, the dimension "generation of knowledge" comprises the creation of new solutions, possibilities, and behavioral patterns. The synthesis of previously separate concepts is a crucial aspect to human creativity. Creative thinking by definition goes beyond existing knowledge but relies on extensive domain-specific and general knowledge.

To proof the suitability of the suggested taxonomy in guiding analysis, we now turn to a description of long-term historic change in human labor that is captured by its categories. Land and physical labor were the principal complementary inputs in the pre-industrial agricultural economy. Before humans attained the ability, *i.e.* the state of technical knowledge, to tap non-human energy sources on a large scale, dynamic human muscular power – as a facet of "mechanical work" – was an important resource and simultaneously constraint on the growth of economic activity [Weissmahr 1992]. After humankind obtained, by means of technological creativity, *i.e.* mental work belonging to the class "generation of knowledge", the knowledge to domesticate animals and to make use of their physical work, human physical labor was substituted by non-anthropogenic energy flows, thereby lowering the physical labor burden, accelerating work, and slightly raising productivity. Before the appearance of waterwheels and windmills, mammals were the major source for "industrial" power beyond human muscle power, for example, for turning grindstones, threshing, and operating water lifts [Diamond 1997, p. 355].

Historical evidence reflects the perpetual struggle of humankind against physical drudgery by means of technical progress [Mokyr 1990]. This is an important motivational driving force behind the accretion of production knowledge. Cordes [2005] suggested that there is an evolved basic want to avoid physical effort beyond a variable individual level of adaptation. Aversive stimuli resulting from these kinds of physiological experience or their observation motivate agents to improve on this situation, for example, via means of technological innovation. This is in line with Peter Corning's bioeconomics approach [2005] that focuses on the relationship between our biologically based motivational substrate and learned and culturally molded behaviors (and institutions) through which these motivations are expressed [p. 232]. His concept of basic needs explicitly aims at opening the "black box" of the individual agent and at explaining individual motivation. The motivations behind our revealed preferences and subjective utility assessments, Corning argues, are directly or indirectly related to meeting our basic needs [see also Cordes 2006].

There are, of course, additional factors that influence the pace of technological change: via a society's incentive structure, also property rights and the institutional setting enable and influence the direction of technological advancement [North and Thomas 1977; North and Weingast 1989]. Consequently, there are two directions of causality: market mechanisms and incentive devices that induce technological advancement as well as human technological creativity that often opens up – without pre-existing price signals – new opportunities that then modify an incentive structure or institutional setting rather than *vice versa.* This second channel of qualitative change is neglected in most (micro-)economic analyzes and necessitates the identification of concrete contents of human preferences and motivations [2].

We argue here that looking at the qualitative structure of labor inputs enables an understanding of aspects of human strivings underlying technological creativity: these labor inputs served as a kind of focusing device, similar to the role of various bottle-necks appearing in the production process [Rosenberg 1969] or that of relative factor prices [Acemoglu 2002]. Of course, also growing markets and evolving organizations accompany economic expan-

2. See Mokyr [1990] for a similar argument concerning the channels of inducement of technological progress [p. 295] and historical evidence.

sion [e.g. Smith 1776/1993]. While these are important factors, other constraints and driving forces that are not reflected in an *ex ante* structure of relative prices play a crucial role. Hence, the claim is that the focus on human labor inputs contributes to an understanding of some essential directions and biases of technical change.

The period from roughly 1000 AD to the close of the fifteenth century witnessed a decisive development in the history of the effort to mechanically harness and direct the forces of nature for human purposes [White Jr. 1962, chap. III]. In late medieval Europe, the watermill became one of the energetic foundations of the contemporary society applying waterpower to a host of tasks. Waterwheels were transformed from a device only used for grinding flour into a ubiquitous source of energy that was utilized on rivers of any type. There were first combinations of these non-human energy flows with sophisticated mechanical devices. By the fourteenth century, European people had made extraordinary progress in their efforts to substitute water- and wind-power for human physical labor in the basic industries [White Jr. 1962, p. 88]. The growth of production was no longer constrained by scarce human physical energy inputs in the form of mechanical work.

Original human work tasks, in this case, heavy physical work, were relieved by or passed over to artificial devices and animals. Instead, mental skills for supervising, attendance, guiding, and caring activities became necessary to a greater extent [Witt 1997], labor qualities that belong to the taxon "utilization of knowledge". In general, more and more facets of mental work were necessary to create and implement the growing contemporary epistemic base of all these technologies, labor inputs that are assigned to the categories "expression of knowledge" and "generation of knowledge". Especially after the invention of the printing press in 1453 by Johannes Gutenberg, information handling abilities as aspects of mental labor qualities became important for a growing proportion of the population, including activities that belong to the taxon "acquisition of knowledge" [e.g. Mokyr 1990, p. 205; Eisenstein 1997]. The storage and distribution of written information became much cheaper than before and the pace of technological evolution increased. More aspects of the function "storage of knowledge" could be transferred from humans to artifacts. It became easier to access the epistemic base of technology and to creatively enhance it by recombining existing pieces of knowledge. At the same time, a – still frugal – knowledge and educational system had to organize and manage the growing amount of technical knowledge, comprising more and more labor services that belong to the category "communication of knowledge".

Contingent on the knowledge about the potential and the economic feasibility to ease or transfer certain sorts of labor to artificial devices (or, in the beginning, to animals), humans were capable of increasing the production volume, easing labor burden, or improving general labor conditions. For example, agricultural technology, such as steel breakers, plows, seed drills, reapers, mowers, and threshers, evolved from rudimentary implements to increasingly sophisticated machinery [David 1975, p. 198]. By and by, these new production techniques greatly enhanced productivity and set free human labor, above all physical labor (first mechanical work, then facets of psychomotor work). The development of harvesting methods proceeded from sickles, via scythes, to grain cradles, and ultimately to mechanical reapers, which could be combined with non-human sources of energy and which mainly require mental labor inputs (belonging to the class "utilization of knowledge").

In the course of the emergence of a domestic rural industry between the sixteenth and nineteenth centuries in many regions of Middle Europe, the attained technical knowledge allowed for a partial substitution of the complementary factors, unskilled labor, raw materials, and capital, for relatively high skilled urban artisans [Cerman and Ogilvie 1996; Goldin and Katz 1998]. Many sophisticated mechanical devices substituted frugal psychomotor work for demanding handicraft by fulfilling their tasks almost automatically. The appearance of these practical achievements was conditioned largely by the mechanical difficulties encountered and the knowledge about mechanical possibilities available at that time [Usher 1954, p. 297]. Predominantly, this machinery still relied on physical energy generated by human agents.

This changed during the Industrial Revolution, when machines that worked rapidly and tirelessly in combination with new non-anthropogenic sources of energy – in the first instance the steam engine – substituted human skill ("demanding handicraft"), time, and physical effort ("mechanical work") on a large scale [Landes 1969, p. 41ff; von Tunzelmann 1995]. Non-creative mental work, such as psychic attention, monitoring, reaction, and supervising of machinery ("utilization of knowledge"), became more significant in the direct process of production. Progress in transportation technologies further lowered the amount of physical labor effort engaged in this field of activity. Many machines, which were employed in the rural domestic industries before, were now further refined and combined with non-human energy sources in centralized factories. Highly developed machine tools replaced even more demanding handicraft and became more and more automatic [e.g. Rosenberg 1963] – a process of deskilling. Technical change during the late eighteenth and early nineteenth centuries has been skill replacing [e.g. Mulligan Jr. 1981].

At the same time, as the epistemic base of production grew, these machines required new, highly specialized occupations in their creation and implementation [e.g. Atack *et alii* 2004], *i.e.* agents that provide labor qualities of the taxa "expression of knowledge" and "generation of knowledge". Increasingly complex instructions and machinery required higher levels of mental skills in surveillance and maintenance ("utilization of knowledge"), while the complementary direct labor inputs to these devices on the shop-floor were frugal ("psychomotor work"). The growing epistemic base of production systems increased the demand for formally educated process engineers, *i.e.* skills connected to the implementation and operation of sophisticated machinery. These developments led to a heightening of the barrier between expert and non-expert labor and a polarization of skills.

Moreover, skills for handling the growing quantity of commercial information that had to be stored, processed, and transmitted gained in importance, for example, in a vast variety of clerical functions [e.g. Greenwood 1997] – aspects of different forms of mental work (e.g. "utilization of knowledge" or "storage of knowledge"). Moreover, a growing educational infrastructure allowed for the attainment of specific skills and knowledge ("acquisition of knowledge") and an efficient dissemination of knowledge ("communication of knowledge"). Technical and scientific education of key segments of the workforce became essential. Finally, from the middle of the 19th century, a growing number of technologies were inspired by scientific advances ("generation of knowledge").

Taken as aggregated figures instead of historical case studies, throughout the whole twentieth century a rapid and persistent secular growth in the demand for more highly educated workers has been demonstrated. New technologies have been skill-biased with an acceleration in the skill-bias beginning in the late 1970s [e.g. Berman and Machin 1995; Chennells and Van Reenen 1999]. The largest and most widespread change in the complementary relationship between skills and technology was caused by information technology. Modern production systems are characterized by a combination of this technology and sophisticated mechanical devices. Moreover, due to these advances in information manipulating technologies, many aspects of non-creative mental work are delegated to artificial devices. Frugal problem-solving procedures ("storage of knowledge" and "utilization of knowledge"), which are applied to well-defined tasks, are executed by computer programs. Work processes are restructured by allocating routine symbol processing tasks to computers while separating out tasks that still require human skills.

Consequently, the spread of computer usage is strongly associated with an overall process of upskilling [e.g. Autor *et alii* 2003; Green *et alii* 2003]. There has been a trend toward a higher ratio of information-processing to goods-handling employment [Castells and Yuko 1994]. Zuboff [1988] termed this development the increasing "abstraction" of work. The linkage of upskilling with computerization is one explanation as to why upskilling has been widespread in the economy, rather than confined to specific industries. However, not all tasks are equally amenable to computerization. Computers contribute to the process of substituting machinery for human labor in routine symbolic processing, *i.e.* to store, retrieve, sort, and act upon information. They perform poorly, however, in tasks requiring developing, drawing inferences from models, solving of new problems, or formulating persuasive arguments.

Information and communication technologies provide manifold opportunities to transfer further elements of mental work involving the acquisition, maintenance, processing, and dissemination of information to electronic automata that then permit a multiplication and acceleration of these work tasks formerly done by humans. Residual labor is likely to be transferred to mental work activities that involve higher cognitive capabilities, especially tasks requiring higher problem solving skills and creativity (e.g. "expression of knowledge" and "generation of knowledge") – a process resulting in upskilling. Moreover, in the course of a growing epistemic base of technology, further knowledge and thus manifestations of mental work are needed to handle the existing knowledge resulting in higher specialization of occupations and more division of knowledge [Mokyr 2002, p. 9]. The necessary coordination and integration of production processes entails a growing number of agents and firms specializing in the organization of transactions between different producers, as well as from producers to consumers. As a general trend in economic evolution, the amount of skills and knowledge that has to be attained, stored, or disseminated ("acquisition of knowledge", "storage of knowledge", and "communication of knowledge"), as well as the amount of creative human labor inputs applied in developing sophisticated machinery and providing products and services has grown.

## 3. Some recurrent patterns in the evolution of labor and technology

As a result of the preceding historical inquiry, a recurrent pattern in economic development is identified: due to technological creativity, humans' learned to successively transfer certain qualities of labor to artificial devices, most of which can be combined with non-human sources of energy. On account of the growing feasibility of first transferring different forms of physical labor and then manifestations of mental work to automata, the requirements on human labor inputs changed, which is reflected in the complementary qualitative structure of employed human capabilities in production.

Since the introduction of the concept of capital-skill-complementarity by Griliches [1969], many post-war econometric studies found that capital, *i.e.* embodied technical knowledge, and skilled labor are complements in production, whereas capital and unskilled labor are substitutes [also Machin and Van Reenen 1998]. In contrast, among many labor historians and in the sociological literature a process of deskilling, *i.e.* a reduction in skill requirements in production, is considered to be a deep trend underlying long-term economic development. Indeed, many historical studies indicate that the capital-skill-complementarity was not a persistent pattern of economic development.

Three patterns of long-term skill change can be distinguished: upskilling, deskilling, or the polarization of skills [Adler 1992]. First, the "upskilling" approach concludes that the automation of manufacturing results in freeing workers from highly routinized tasks and in creating more integrated work processes including more aspects of mental work inputs [Piore and Sabel 1984; Zuboff 1988]. Second, followers of the "deskilling" approach argue that market forces urge employers to continuously simplify the labor of skilled occupations. The process of deskilling, it is argued, is not confined to manual work: also non-manual – particularly clerical – work has been substantially deskilled by technological advancement [Braverman 1974; Crompton and Jones 1984]. The third position combines elements of the first two by postulating an increasing polarization of the workforce. Some employees benefit from technological advancement through an increase in skill levels, while others are trapped in low skilled forms of employment [e.g. Gallie 1991; Autor *et alii* 2006].

The historical material provides evidence for all these trends in the development of labor. However, the perspective on the development of human labor and the epistemic base of production proposed here gives an alternative account for skill-biased or unskilled-biased technological change and its implications. The qualitative aspects of technology and labor come to the fore. In this context, the heterogeneity of skills – as captured by the proposed taxonomy of human labor inputs – is central for the analysis of these empirical regularities:

> *Proposition 1*: Depending on the attained technical knowledge about the transferability of certain sorts of labor to artificial devices and about the possibilities to tap non-human energy sources, instances of upskilling, deskilling, or polarization of the workforce occurred in economic development.

This proposition contains important facets of qualitative, historical change: the concrete economic implications of these transfers only become comprehensible when the production factor labor is disaggregated. Given the historical evidence, such a disaggregation should be finer grained than those applied in standard microeconomic analysis. Moreover, the transfer opportunities opened up in the course of time, *i.e.* new technological knowledge, changed the complementary labor inputs at every point in history. Therefore, for most of the time, there rather was a sequence of different complementary human contributions than static situations characterized by substitutional relations between labor inputs and capital in which these factors could easily react to price signals. Finally, different sorts of human labor have been in the focus of technological advancement at different points in time depending on the previously attained technical knowledge and emerging "bottlenecks" – an aspect of path-dependent economic change. The qualitative structure of labor inputs also acts as a focusing device for the further generation of technical knowledge [Rosenberg 1969].

For instance, Braverman's [1974] analysis of deskilling processes is correct regarding many of the direct consequences of the growing epistemic base of production during the nineteenth century. But, on the other hand, he underestimates the repercussions of the new knowledge base on the skill demands in relation to constructing, maintaining, and implementing this machinery ("expression of knowledge", "generation of knowledge") and with respect to the societal knowledge system that has to accumulate, store, and disseminate this knowledge ("acquisition of knowledge", "communication of knowledge"). Moreover, although computerization entails aggregate upskilling, it may be combined with the deskilling of single jobs. Here, a differentiation between "white collar" and "blue collar" employees does not depict instances of, for example, deskilling in clerical occupations.

Further implications of these processes can be shown:

> *Proposition 2*: The possibility to ease or replace a certain quality of human labor with mechanical appliances or electronic automata permitted a multiplication and acceleration of tasks formerly done by humans. The resulting productivity gains triggered periods of strong economic growth and/or enabled population growth.

Again, for an understanding of these historical processes, it is insufficient to just differentiate between two – substitutable – sorts of human labor. Instead, the more detailed taxonomy of human labor inputs directs attention to the concrete human contributions that became subject to the endeavors of transferring them to machines and it facilitates a deeper understanding of economic implications entailed by these instances of labor replacements.

The accumulation of production knowledge also offers an endogenous source of knowledge-driven growth that accounts for a temporarily accelerating pace of technological progress [see also Witt 2004]. This dynamic is captured by the following proposition:

> *Proposition 3*: New production knowledge enabled a reduction in working time for the same output and set free spare human time and effort for the systematic search for, and application of, further innovations in tools, appliances, and energy uses that again raised productivity and shortened working times [3].

A prerequisite for these self-augmenting economic developments are innovative activities within the economy that facilitate a successive transfer of labor to machines setting free human

3. Such a process that feeds back on itself as a recurrent feature of historical economic development is not amenable to the analytical tools of standard growth or production theory. Substitutability between factors of production and corresponding price signals are not the crucial features of this autocatalytic dynamic.

cognitive capacities. The taxonomy of human labor reflects the steps toward releasing parts of the population from spending the bulk of their time performing physical work that enabled humankind to generate and apply ever-more knowledge, *i.e.* to provide more and more work inputs belonging to the categories "expression of knowledge" and "generation of knowledge". Of course, the released working time also could be, and has been, spent on leisure or consumption that delays a potential growth of the economy. Moreover, population growth may prevent per capita income from increasing during these periods. However, if it is spent on knowledge creation and learning/education (taxon "acquisition of knowledge"), a kind of autocatalytic cycle can result that causes an increasing growth rate.

In this context, the growth of research employment is not driven by population growth [as, e.g. *in* Kortum 1997], but by the release of parts of the workforce from performing certain kinds of labor. Hence, the accumulation of production knowledge itself creates – via increases of productivity – the prerequisites for its further expansion. This line of argument differs from established models of endogenous technological change, such as Aghion and Howitt [1992], Grossman and Helpman [1991], and Romer [1986], where one implication is that high population spurs technological change due to the nonrivalry of knowledge.

The dynamics of economies over long periods experience significant long-term variations in their aggregate performance [e.g. Kuznets 1940; Rosenberg and Frischtak 1983]. The successive transfer of human labor to machines can constitute long cycles in economic growth that exhibit the effects of the above-mentioned autocatalytic development. Freeman and Perez [1988] have suggested some characteristics of these successive long growth waves: first, they identify the "early mechanization wave" of the 1770s to 1840s. Sophisticated mechanical devices enabled the substitution of demanding handicraft for frugal psychomotor work. Second, during their "steam power and railway wave" of the 1840s to 1890s machines and new sources of energy substituted for human skill and physical effort on a large scale. Third, during the "electrical and heavy engineering wave" of the 1890s to 1940s, electromechanical devices replaced more complex forms of demanding handicraft by (semi-)automatic machines. During a fourth "Fordist mass production wave" from the 1940s to 1980s production became more routinized, unskilled labor was employed on extensive machinery that was easy to operate, and massive gains in productivity were enabled. A last "information and communication wave" from the 1980s entailed advances in information manipulating technologies that made possible the delegation of facets of human non-creative mental labor (e.g. "storage of knowledge" and – in the case of routine tasks – "utilization of knowledge") to artificial devices associated with an acceleration and multiplication of these tasks setting free human cognitive resources. These are the ingredients of an endogenous autocatalytic economic development that manifests itself in an accelerating pace of technological progress during certain periods of time. These findings reconcile the observation that countries with more educated workers grow faster with the fact that sheer population size does not promote growth when crucial prerequisites for such an autocatalytic growth of knowledge are missing.

## 4. Some political implications

Some regularities in the development of human labor and the epistemic base of technology have been presented in the preceding sections. This qualitative change also contributes to the selective process of recognizing policy problems. The growing knowledge about the transferability of certain sorts of human labor gave – and still gives – rise to new policy problems and political desiderata. Technological progress voids certain kinds of labor and necessitates the provision of others, as has been stated by proposition 1. It also changes working conditions, values, and aspiration levels of subjects; processes that ultimately express themselves in political concerns.

The continuous generation and accretion of production knowledge depends in essence on human cognitive capabilities, *i.e.* facets of mental work inputs. As has been suggested by proposition 3, the release of parts of the workforce from performing certain sorts of labor enabled humankind to spend this time in the search for further technical innovations, *i.e.* the generation and application of ever-more knowledge, making possible the transfer of more human labor qualities to machines. It also follows that the knowledge-content of the production process as a whole increases in the course of time due to more and more work effort spend on generating and expressing knowledge.

The public or private provision of an educational infrastructure and the institutionalization of scientific research and development were fundamental for this kind of autocatalytic economic development to occur. A subsequent policy problem was the adaptation of this system to an increasing pace of innovative activity and new demands on skill formation due to a growing knowledge-content of labor as a consequence of the effects of propositions 1 and 3. Currently, many advanced countries face the challenge to reform their social security systems as well as the fiscal systems in order to account for longer periods of education and higher wage differentials in the course of an individual's working life. Pension schemes have to be changed given the fact that life-working times are dwindling for an increasing number of people due to extended periods of education before the occupational career and further vocational training throughout working life. Furthermore, the arrangement of a fiscal system must take into account that people experience long unpaid periods of education followed by periods of far above average earnings. The latter contribute to a "cross-subsidization" of the former; tax rates have to make this inter-temporal income transfer possible. Altogether, the social and fiscal systems should enable agents to switch between periods of work and further training to keep pace with the growing knowledge-content of tasks remaining to humans.

An implicit prediction of many endogenous growth models – and thus an issue for many policy makers – is that growth rates should exhibit large permanent increases [e.g. Romer 1994; Jones, 1995]. According to our argument, the mechanisms underlying the autocatalytic increase of production knowledge do not necessarily entail this: technological breakthroughs concerning the transfer of human labor to machines may become increasingly hard to find in the course of technological advancement. Moreover, the amount of knowledge that has to be attained before an agent has reached the knowledge frontier and is able to contribute new pieces of knowledge to the existing stock is growing [Kortum 1997]. Hence, more and more educational effort is necessary to enable agents to attain, handle, and coordinate the existing stock of knowledge, *i.e.* an increasing part of this effort is absorbed without raising an economy's growth rate [4]. Although the growth of knowledge exhibits autocatalytic characteristics during some periods, economic growth rates do not increase permanently because the foundation of this self-augmenting growth – the increasing availability of human mental work capacities – also finally sets boundaries to this development.

Given the fact that there is no universal metric for the production factor "knowledge", empirical inquiries into its effects face severe problems. The insight that knowledge is not a self-contained factor of production, but embodied by other factors – human labor and capital in changing (complementary) compositions – offers a solution to this problem. The taxonomy of human labor and the subsequent qualitative analysis of changing human inputs to production show the characteristics of different labor inputs, their knowledge content, and which of these contributions are – including their knowledge-content – transferred to artificial devices in the course of historical time. This perspective opens a way how to indirectly measure knowledge brought to production via human labor and capital.

Labor qualities and their cognitive foundations connected to the handling of knowledge, such as the acquisition, storage, utilization, communication, expression as well as the generation of knowledge (as systematized by the taxonomy), played an increasingly important role in the course of technological progress. Again, some of these functions were completely or partly transferred to machines, for example, the storing and communicating of know-

4. This explains some of the paradoxes in Jones [Jones, 1995], where growing education expenditures do not trigger proportional economic growth.

ledge, thereby influencing productivity development – an aspect captured by proposition 2. This shifting qualitative structure in the realm of mental labor inputs mainly causes an upskilling of the workforce (proposition 1). This qualitative composition of labor partly determines the prices of commodities that depend, to a great extent, on the knowledge-content of human labor inputs necessary for their production and on the amount and kind of production knowledge that can be employed while embodied by machines. Moreover, the qualitative structure of labor inputs and their corresponding knowledge-contents explain much of the structure of wages in an economy. Many tasks that are currently non-transferable, for example, creative work inputs, are knowledge-rich and yield high incomes. On the other hand, machines that embody a certain kind of knowledge can leave knowledge-poor and low wage performances to humans – a potentially deskilling effect within an overall trend toward more skilled labor and a potential explanation for increasing wage differentials and connected social problems. An increasing capital intensity in production often entails greater wage differentials due to different degrees of transferability of the various qualities of human labor and their respective knowledge-contents to machines.

Furthermore, disaggregating human labor shows that we may not only observe a secular trend toward the service sector as predicted by Fourastié [1976]. Instead, we also witness the changing complementary inputs of certain human labor qualities and capital goods that incorporate the attained production knowledge. This perspective is superior in grasping intra-sectoral qualificational developments and changing shares of sectors in national income. The taxonomy of human labor may even serve as a starting point for devising an alternative division of sectors in an economy. This is relevant for economic policy making, for example, as to qualification tendencies of the workforce, increasing social inequality including income shares and wages, or the development of an economy's sectoral composition and connected employment effects that may call for political action.

Moreover, some of the human cognitive capacities systematized in the taxonomy of human labor inputs have been or will be constraints to an ongoing knowledge growth process. One important cognitive constraint of economic development is the time intensive acquisition of knowledge by humans that is indispensable again and again in every generation. New technologies, methods, or procedures that facilitate a more efficient or convenient passing on and absorption of knowledge can be expected to be conducive to economic performance. Another bottleneck are human creative problem solving capabilities that are required to an increasing extent due to an accelerating pace of technological advancement (proposition 3) as well as more and more problems arising from this advancement [Rosenberg 1969]. The solutions to these problems again cause subsequent problems necessitating even more not transferable creative labor inputs to handle this self-augmenting development. These capabilities presuppose a high level of education and should be fostered early within a country's educational system. As far as market forces fail to account for such problems, it is a task for policy makers to identify these arising problems to adequately allocate means for public research, public procurement, and to recognize the demand for legislative measures.

The changing qualitative structure of labor inputs has far reaching repercussions on the behavior of the labor supply side. Here, it is the family that provides human labor in changing qualities. As shown by the historical analysis and the taxonomy of labor in section 2, in the pre-industrial agricultural economy physical labor was the dominant quality of human labor employed in production and provided by the family. After humankind had learned to combine mechanical devices with non-human sources of energy, the (knowledge-poor) physical aspects of human labor became less important. Instead, further aspects of mental work were required as labor inputs and a growing educational infrastructure allowed the attainment of specific skills and knowledge. Now, the family had to provide support for its members to enable them to utilize this infrastructure in order to acquire the endowment with mental working capabilities. Higher mental capabilities and a growing amount of knowledge are acquired in continually longer periods of special education at the beginning and throughout lifelong working time, which is a direct implication of the autocatalytic process described by proposition 3. Hence, the role and the structure of the family changed: family members do not start early in life to contribute to a family's income, instead they require its support for increasing periods of education. This changed the demographic structure, especially with respect to the number of children. Parents invest more time in their own education and thus postpone their reproductive efforts, while they also spend more resources to enable their fewer children to attain a profound education [5]. It is with respect to the acquisition of knowledge that politics can provide effective support for the family to enable its members to utilize the educational infrastructure. These are domains where political intervention can solve problems that are unlikely to be tackled by, for example, imperfect real-world credit markets.

Also in the field of manual work there are challenges for politics and the private households. In the case of relatively unique products, there is often little mechanization of production. Much work is done by hand, frequently involving demanding handicraft and the utilization of sophisticated machinery that assists this work ("utilization of knowledge" in the taxonomy), both hinting at the importance of a system of extended elementary schools and vocational training for these occupations. Policies on skill formation in these fields are important means for governments to encounter some profound changes in the labor market and to exploit employment opportunities [Green *et alii* 2003]. Again, the evolution of the epistemic base of technology necessitates the provision of changing qualities of human labor by the households. On the other hand, the quality of labor provided by the households also influences the evolution of technology due to the fact that well-educated agents constitute a market for sophisticated machinery [Acemoglu 1998].

Economic growth theory and most of aggregate production theory deem skilled labor to be a more or less perfect substitute for unskilled labor and both to be substitutable with capital [Galor and Moav 2000; Hamermesh 1996]. In an equilibrium framework,

5. For these developments and the role of contraceptives in this context see also Goldin [2006].

the skill-biased technological change over the past 60 years and the unskilled biased technological progress during the late eighteenth and early nineteenth centuries, as exemplary cases, are explained by referring to reversible price and market size effects [Acemoglu 2002]. Although price and market size effects – among other factors – play an important role as focusing devices for technological change, they are not part of easily reversible equilibrium results: according to our historical, qualitative approach, the growing knowledge about the transferability of certain kinds of human labor to artificial devices crucially determines the complementary qualitative structure of labor employed in production. Simple substitutability between the various forms of labor depicted in the taxonomy and between labor and capital does not exist within a technological regime. Furthermore, from the interplay of effects described by propositions 1 and 3 it follows that the knowledge-content of activities left to humans increases in the course of time. As a result, the effects of relative factor prices on relative demand for skills are secondary to technological characteristics[6]. For this kind of irreversible, qualitative change in historical time, an extension of economists' ahistorical analytical tool-box is inevitable to provide adequate policy advice.

A question of outstanding political importance is whether the gains in higher mental work will compensate for the losses of employment in lower mental and physical work. It is safe to say that employment in the transmission, generation, and application of the epistemic base of technology will increase, which follows from proposition 3. Moreover, the necessity of attaining more and more knowledge before and during one's work life can be a reason for altogether shorter periods of time spent on the workplace and may thus have an employment effect. In service employment there are – given the current technological knowledge – many jobs that

6. For example, the alteration of relative factor costs neither noticeably influenced the pace of productivity increases nor induced a variation in the process of production toward a more labor-intensive way of manufacturing [Kelly 2000]. However, on the other hand, relative price can act as a focusing device for the search of innovations [Rosenberg 1969].

are resistant to mechanization. At the moment, the number of these jobs is growing, thereby providing employment opportunities [7]. Due to the fact that skill requirements are low in many of these jobs, this development may give rise – in combination with the above-mentioned upskilling tendencies – to polarization tendencies in the workforce [for empirical evidence see Autor *et alii* 2006].

## 5. Conclusions

This paper has delivered an analysis of qualitative change in the realm of human labor in mutual dependence with the evolution of the epistemic base of technology. With the help of selected historical material and a taxonomy of labor inputs, the role of various types of human capabilities in long-term economic development has been presented along with their interplay with technological advancement. Historically, an outstanding recurrent pattern of socio-economic evolution has been identified: humans learned to ease certain sorts of labor by applying tools. What is more, they found ways to successively transfer qualities of human labor to artificial devices that can be combined with non-human energy sources, a process that started with tools and ended up with automata that are even capable of adopting cognitive tasks from human agents. Therefore, in the long-run, economic evolution may be considered as a sequence of switches between regimes in which the knowledge about the potential and the economic feasibility to transfer certain sorts of labor to artificial devices is mirrored in a characteristic complementary structure of employed labor qualities in production. The possibility of easing or replacing a certain quality of labor with mechanical appliances and electronic automata permitted a multiplication and acceleration of respective tasks.

Moreover, it has been demonstrated that the release of parts of the workforce from performing certain sorts of labor enabled

7. In this context, a reduction of wages can have positive employment effects. Social problems associated with such wage cuts can give rise to other political concerns.

humankind to spend this time and effort for the search for further technical innovations, *i.e.* the generation and application of evermore knowledge, again raising productivity and setting free working time. A prerequisite for and a consequence of this kind of autocatalytic economic development is the establishment of an educational infrastructure and the institutionalization of research and development providing and absorbing human cognitive capabilities necessary for the handling of a growing stock of societal knowledge. Hence, a permanent challenge to policy makers is the adaptation of the economic system to an increasing pace of innovative activity and new demands on skill formation due to a growing knowledge-content of labor. In addition, some human cognitive capacities have been or will be constraints to this ongoing knowledge growth process. Additional political implications concerning the role of the family in providing certain qualities of labor and further employment effects of technical change have been discussed.

Social scientists have been eager to develop a general theory concerning the impact of technological change on skill structure. However, the quest for one general trend grasping all the ramifications of technology on upskilling, deskilling, or polarization has not been successful. This paper has shown how technology and skill structure coevolve. One argument was that the knowledge about the transferability of certain sorts of labor to artificial devices is crucial in determining the complementary skill structure of labor and thus incidents of upskilling, deskilling, or polarization of the workforce (there is an ongoing debate on this topic based on contradicting wage-based empirical evidence, see, e.g. Acemoglu [2002], Autor *et alii* [2006], and Lemieux [2006]). The observation that the relationship between technology and the qualitative structure of labor is a largely complementary one has direct political implications: it is unlikely that purely price or wage oriented political labor market measures will mitigate the problem of unemployment. This is due to the fact that the different qualities of human labor do not stand in a simple substitutional relationship to each other and to the other means of production and thus do not react to price changes as standard theory predicts.

## REFERENCES

ACEMOGLU D., 1998, "Why do new Technologies Complement Skills? Directed Technical Change and Wage Inequality", *Quarterly Journal of Economics*, vol. CXIII, Issue 4, pp. 1055-1089.

–, 2002, "Directed Technical Change", *Review of Economic Studies*, vol. 69, n° 4, pp. 781-809.

ADLER P.S. (ed.), 1992, *Technology and the Future of Work*, Oxford, Oxford UP.

AGHION Ph. and HOWITT P., 1992, "A Model of Growth Through Creative Destruction", *Econometrica*, vol. 60, n° 2, pp. 323-351.

ATACK J., BATEMAN F. and MARGO R.A., 2004, "Skill Intensity and Rising Wage Dispersion in Nineteenth-Century American Manufacturing", *Journal of Economic History*, vol. 64, n° 1, pp. 172-192.

AUTOR D.H., KATZ L.F. and KEARNEY M.S., 2006, "The Polarization of the U.S. Labor Market", *American Economic Review*, vol. 96, n° 2, pp. 189-194.

—, LEVY F. and MURNANE R.J., 2003, "The Skill Content of Recent Technological Change: An Empirical Exploration", *Quarterly Journal of Economics*, vol. 118, n° 4, pp. 1279-1333.

BECKER G.S., 1993, *Human Capital*, Chicago, University of Chicago Press.

BERMAN E. and MACHIN S., 1995, "Skill Biased Technological Change and the Structure of Employment", *in* S. Dowrick (ed.), *Economic Approaches to Innovation*, Vermont, Edward Elgar, pp. 189-208.

BLOOM B.S., 1969, *Taxonomy of Educational Objectives: The Classification of Educational Goals*, Handbook I, *Cognitive Domain*, New York, McKay.

BRAVERMAN H., 1974, *Labor and Monopoly Capital*, New York, Monthly Review Press.

CASTELLS M. and YUKO A., 1994, "Paths Towards the Informational Society: Employment Structure in G-7 Countries, 1920-90", *International Labour Review*, vol. 133, n° 1, pp. 5-33.

CERMAN M. and OGILVIE S.C., 1996, "Proto-Industrialization, Economic Development and Social Change in Early Modern Europe", *in* M. Cerman and S.C. Ogilvie (eds.), *European Proto-Industrialization*, Cambridge, Cambridge UP, pp. 227-239.

CHENNELLS L. and VAN REENEN J., 1999, "Has Technology Hurt Less Skilled Workers? An Econometric Survey of the Effects of Technical Change on the Structure of Pay and Jobs", *The Institute for Fiscal Studies*, Working Paper Series n° W99/27.

CORDES Ch., 2005, "Long-term Tendencies in Technological Creativity: A Preference-based Approach", *Journal of Evolutionary Economics*, vol. 15, n° 2, pp. 149-168.

–, 2006, "Review of Peter Corning's book 'Holistic Darwinism: Synergy, Cybernetics and the Bioeconomics of Evolution'", *Review of Economic Philosophy*, vol. 2, n° 14, pp. 85-93.

CROMPTON R. and Jones G., 1984, *White-Collar Proletariat*, London, Macmillan Press.

CORNING P.A., 2005, *Holistic Darwinism*, Chicago, University of Chicago Press.

DAVID P.A., 1975, *Technical Choice, Innovation and Economic Growth*, Cambridge, Cambridge UP

DIAMOND J., 1997, *Guns, Germs and Steel*, London, Vintage.

EISENSTEIN E.L., 1997, *The Printing Press as an Agent of Change*, Cambridge, Cambridge UP.

FLEISHMAN Ed.A. and REILLY M.E., 1992, *Handbook of Human Abilities: Definitions, Measurements, and Job Task Requirements*, Palo Alto, Consulting Psychologists Press.

FOURASTIÉ J., 1976, *Le grand espoir du XX^e^ siècle*, Paris, Gallimard.

FREEMAN Ch. and PEREZ C., 1988, "Structural Crises of Adjustment, Business Cycles and Investment Behavior", *in* G. Dosi, C. Freeman, R.R. Nelson, G. Silverberg and L. Soete (eds.), *Technical Change and Economic Theory*, London, Pinter Publishers, pp. 38-66.

GALLIE D., 1991, "Patterns of Skill Change: Upskilling, Deskilling or the Polarization of Skills", *Work, Employment & Society*, vol. 5, n° 3, pp. 319-351.

GALOR O. and MOAV O., 2000, "Ability-biased Technological Transition, Wage Inequality, and Economic Growth", *Quarterly Journal of Economics*, vol. 115, n° 2, pp. 469-497.

GOLDIN Cl., 2006, "The Quiet Revolution That Transformed Women's Employment, Education, and Family", *American Economic Review*, vol. 96, n° 2, pp. 1-21.

— and KATZ L.F., 1998, "The Origins of Technology-Skill Complementarity", *Quarterly Journal of Economics*, vol. 113, n° 3, pp. 693-732.

GREEN F., FELSTAED A. and GALLIE D., 2003, "Computers and the Changing Skill-intensity of Jobs", *Applied Economics*, vol. 35, pp. 1561-1576.

GREENWOOD J., 1997, *The Third Industrial Revolution*, Washington D.C., AEI Press.

GRILICHES Z., 1969, “Capital-Skill Complementarity”, *Review of Economics and Statistics*, vol. 51, n° 4, pp. 465-468.

GROSSMAN G.M. and HELPMAN E., 1991, *Innovation and Growth in the Global Economy*, Cambridge (Mass.), MIT Press.

HAMERMESH D.S., 1996, *Labor Demand*, Princeton, Princeton UP.

JONES Ch.I., 1995, “Time Series Tests of Endogenous Growth Models”, *Quarterly Journal of Economics*, vol. 110, n° 2, pp. 495-525.

KELLY G.M., 2000, “Employment and Concepts of Work in the New Global Economy”, *International Labour Review*, vol. 139, n° 1, pp. 5-32.

KORTUM S.S., 1997, “Research, Patenting, and Technological Change”, *Econometrica*, vol. 65, n° 6, pp. 1389-1419.

KUZNETS S., 1940, “Schumpeter's Business Cycles”, *American Economic Review*, vol. 30, n° 2, pp. 257-271.

LANDES D.S., 1969, *The Unbound Prometheus*, Cambridge, Cambridge UP.

LEMIEUX Th., 2006, “Increasing Residual Wage Inequality: Composition Effects, Noisy Data, or Rising Demand for Skill?”, *American Economic Review*, vol. 96, n° 3, pp. 461-498.

MACHIN S. and VAN REENEN J., 1998, “Technology and Changes in Skill Structure: Evidence from Seven OECD Countries”, *Quarterly Journal of Economics*, vol. 113, n° 4, pp. 1215-1244.

MOKYR Joel, 1990, *The Lever of Riches: Technological Creativity and Economic Progress*, Oxford, Oxford UP.

–, 2002, *The Gifts of Athena. Historical Origins of the Knowledge Economy*, Princeton, Princeton UP.

MULLIGAN W.H. Jr., 1981, “Mechanization and Work in the American Shoe Industry: Lynn, Massachusetts, 1852-1883”, *Journal of Economic History*, vol. 41, n° 1, pp. 59-63.

NORTH D.C. and THOMAS R.P., 1977, “The First Economic Revolution”, *Economic History Review*, vol. 30, n° 2, pp. 229-241.

— and WEINGAST B.R., 1989, “Constitutions and Commitment: The Evolution of Institutional Governing Public Choice in Seventeenth-Century England”, *Journal of Economic History*, vol. 49, n° 4, pp. 803-832.

PIORE M.J. and SABEL Ch.F., 1984, *The Second Industrial Divide*, New York, Basic Books.

ROMER P.M., 1986, “Increasing Returns and Long-Run Growth”, *Journal of Political Economy*, vol. 94, pp. 1002-1037.

–, 1994, “The Origins of Endogenous Growth”, *Journal of Economic Perspectives*, vol. 8, n° 1, pp. 3-22.

ROSENBERG N., 1963, "Technological Change in the Machine Tool Industry, 1840-1910", *Journal of Economic History*, vol. 23, n° 4, pp. 414-443.

–, 1969, "The Direction of Technological Change: Inducement Mechanisms and Focusing Devices", *Economic Development and Cultural Change*, vol. 18, n° 1, pp. 1-24.

— and FRISCHTAK Cl.R., 1983, "Long Waves and Economic Growth: A Critical Appraisal", *American Economic Review*, vol. 73, n° 2, pp. 146-151.

SMITH A., 1993 (1776), *An Inquiry into the Nature and Causes of the Wealth of Nations*, Oxford, Oxford UP.

USHER A.P., 1954, *A History of Mechanical Inventions*, Cambridge, Harvard UP.

VON TUNZELMANN N.G., 1995, "Time-Saving Technical Change: The Cotton Industry in the English Industrial Revolution", *Explorations in Economic History*, vol. 32, pp. 1-27.

WEISSMAHR J.A., 1992, "The Factors of Production of Evolutionary Economics", *in* U. Witt (ed.), *Explaining Process and Change: Approaches to Evolutionary Economics*, Ann Arbor, University of Michigan Press, pp. 67-79.

WHITE L. Jr., 1962, *Medieval Technology and Social Change*, Oxford, Oxford UP.

WITT U., 1997, "Self-Organization and Economics – What is New?", *Structural Change and Economic Dynamics*, vol. 8, pp. 489-507.

–, 2004, "On the Proper Interpretation of 'Evolution' in Economics and its Implications for Production Theory", *Journal of Economic Methodology*, vol. 11, n° 2, pp. 125-146.

ZUBOFF Sh., 1988, *In the Age of the Smart Machine*, New York, Basic Books.

# RECENSION D'OUVRAGE

Karl Polanyi, *Essais*
Textes réunis et présentés par Michèle Cangiani et Jérôme Maucourant
Paris, Seuil, 2008


## BÉNÉDICTE ZIMMERMANN *


Ce volume rassemble quarante trois textes de Karl Polanyi jusqu'alors inaccessibles en langue française. Traduits de l'allemand par Françoise Laroche et de l'anglais par Laurence Collaud, les morceaux choisis, dont certains sont des inédits, couvrent quarante quatre ans de production intellectuelle de 1922 à 1966.

L'architecture du livre présente les textes dans un ordre qui ne suit pas forcément celui de leur écriture. Elle met en œuvre une double chronologie : d'une part, la chronologie de l'objet, à savoir la forme et la place de l'économie dans les sociétés de l'antiquité à la période contemporaine, d'autre part, la chronologie du cheminement de la pensée de Polanyi. La restitution de la date de chaque texte dans la table des matières permet au lecteur d'évoluer au gré de cette double entrée. Il convient de saluer ce travail d'édition qui rend compte tout à la fois de l'ampleur et la cohérence d'une œuvre et de sa logique de construction.

La première partie, dédiée aux « économies primitives et archaïques » réunit les textes les plus tardifs (de 1946 à 1966) et


* EHESS/CRIA, 96 bd Raspail, 75006 Paris, Bzim@ehess.fr.

approfondit, études détaillées à l'appui, la thèse, déjà avancée en 1944 dans *La grande transformation*, de l'historicité de l'économie de marché et du capitalisme comme formes spécifiques d'institutionnalisation de l'économie. La deuxième partie donne accès, à travers des écrits datés de 1922 à 1947, à une analyse sur le vif de la crise de l'économie de marché entre la Première et la Seconde Guerre mondiale. Elle place le socialisme soviétique et la montée en puissance des fascismes européens au cœur de la réflexion. La biographie intellectuelle de l'essayiste, qui cherche à comprendre les ressorts du totalitarisme et du nazisme, s'y mêle intimement à la biographie du citoyen originaire d'une famille juive qui, converti au christianisme, fut un théoricien actif de la gauche chrétienne dans les années 1930 (chap. 32). Enfin, la dernière partie réunit des textes écrits après 1945, à la tonalité plus prospective. Elle pose le diagnostic de la fin de l'économie de marché et identifie les conditions de son dépassement en vue d'une société plus humaine, faisant de la liberté un enjeu décisif.

Prises ensemble les différentes parties illustrent l'éclectisme de la pensée de Polanyi. D'abord sur le plan des disciplines : outre l'économie sont conviées l'histoire, l'anthropologie, la philosophie et la science politique. Ensuite sur le plan de la diversité des domaines d'investigation qui vont de l'organisation économique et politique du Dahomey au XVIIIe siècle à la constitution fasciste de l'Autriche en passant par l'histoire de la monnaie coquillage cauri. L'analyse de l'articulation entre l'économie et le politique, à travers le temps et dans différentes sociétés, constitue le fil conducteur entre ces terrains d'investigation variés. Partant du constat de la pathologie de l'articulation entre économie et politique sous la forme démocratie/capitalisme des années 1920/1930, Polanyi cherche dans le passé la marque du caractère historiquement construit de cette forme pour mieux projeter dans le futur les conditions de son dépassement. Il en résulte une économie politique qui marie la rigueur de l'analyse scientifique à l'expression de convictions éthiques. Le trait remarquable de ce projet intellectuel est que les préoccupations éthiques et politiques n'y occultent jamais la complexité socio-historique, mais se nourrissent au contraire d'une connaissance approfondie de ses expressions contrastées et singulières, faisant preuve d'un véritable sens de l'enquête de détail.

A partir d'études d'anthropologie historique, la première partie montre que le commerce, le marché et la monnaie ne sont pas nécessairement destinés à fonctionner ensemble. La distinction posée au chapitre 6 entre la définition institutionnelle du commerce et sa version marchande est ici essentielle. « D'un point de vue *institutionnel*, le commerce est une méthode qui consiste à acquérir des biens qui ne sont pas disponibles sur place. [...] Dans sa *définition marchande*, le commerce est le mouvement des biens qui vont entrer dans le marché, c'est-à-dire qu'il est une institution qui comporte un mécanisme offre-demande-prix » (p. 119). Polanyi distingue trois types de commerce – par don, par traité et marchand – avant d'identifier les conditions du basculement du commerce, au sens large, au marché. L'apparition de la monnaie, définie comme « objets durables qu'on peut quantifier soit en les comptant soit en les mesurant » (p. 211), joue un rôle décisif dans ce processus. Toutefois, comme il l'a fait pour le commerce, Polanyi soutient à l'exemple de la monnaie coquillage cauri que l'apparition de la monnaie n'est pas nécessairement liée au marché, mais peut aussi être le résultat d'objectifs politiques de consolidations de l'organisation sociale et de l'État. Cette première partie met en évidence les apports d'une approche institutionnaliste qui défend la thèse de l'encastrement de l'économie dans la société et de l'importance des institutions non-économiques pour comprendre l'économie. En considérant l'économie sous l'angle d'un procès institutionnalisé susceptible de prendre différentes formes, cette approche distingue l'économie en générale de sa forme capitaliste orientée vers le gain et le profit. Mais Polanyi montre aussi que dans la société de marché, c'est la société qui en vient à être encastrée dans l'économie plutôt que l'inverse. Le capitalisme et ses normes irriguent alors l'ensemble des institutions sociales pour générer un processus de renforcement mutuel ; processus que Polanyi semble paradoxalement sous-estimer lorsqu'il diagnostique après la Seconde Guerre mondiale la fin de l'économie de marché.

La thèse dominante de la deuxième partie est celle de l'autonomisation, jusqu'à l'incompatibilité, entre démocratie et économie dans les pays industrialisés de l'Europe continentale de l'entre-deux-guerres (chap. 19). D'un côté, le bolchévisme annexe l'économie au politique, de l'autre le fascisme absorbe le politique dans un corporatisme économique ; dans les deux cas la démocratie est la grande perdante. « Aujourd'hui, l'économie manque tout autant de culture politique que la politique de culture économique » (p. 355). Polanyi voit dans ce divorce le symptôme d'une crise profonde et irréversible de la société de marché. Il intègre de manière tout à fait originale la Première Guerre mondiale dans l'analyse de cette crise qu'il ne conçoit pas sous un seul angle économique, mais dans une double perspective économique et politique (chap. 18).

Tout en portant sur des évènements du passé, les textes de cette seconde partie articulent des réflexions d'ordre plus générales dont l'actualité, dépouillée des ornements désuets du passé, reste entière. C'est le cas des pages introductives au chapitre sur la comptabilité socialiste (chap. 15) qui thématisent les tensions entre « l'évaluation sociale » des biens et leur « évaluation individuelle » (p. 293). Alors que le consommateur individuel privilégie le prix, l'esthétique, la qualité, la quantité ou la commodité d'usage du produit fini, l'évaluation social prend en compte le processus de production et ses conditions, ses effets humains, sociaux et environnementaux. Selon l'étalon choisi, la valeur d'usage d'un même bien s'en trouve profondément altérée. Dans un autre chapitre (17), Polanyi reprend cette problématique sous l'angle de la tension entre producteur et consommateur, sachant qu'une même personne est bien souvent et l'un et l'autre. Ce déplacement lui permet de montrer que le dilemme n'est pas entre l'individu et le collectif, mais qu'il habite chaque personne dont les différents rôles (« fonctions » dans la terminologie polanyienne) font le siège d'intérêts contradictoires. Polanyi en appelle à l'éveil du producteur, du consommateur et du citoyen qui sommeillent en chacun de nous, à la prise de conscience de leurs contradictions et à la responsabilisation de l'un par rapport à l'autre. Un tel idéal d'une économie consciente d'elle-même, soumise à une évaluation individuelle *et* sociale est aujourd'hui plus que jamais d'actualité non seulement en matière d'écologie et de développement durable, mais également de justice sociale.

Cette topique de la prise de conscience et de la responsabilité trouve ses prolongements dans la dernière partie à visée plus prospective. Polanyi y analyse les conditions d'une société nouvelle à même de concilier démocratie et économie ; une société qui ne serait plus gouvernée par la fiction de la marchandise qui envahit toutes les sphères de la vie (chap. 37), une société où le rang et le statut ne seraient pas déterminés au premier chef par le revenu. Convaincu que le socialisme annonce une nouvelle civilisation, Polanyi considère la mentalité de marché obsolète. « Au XIX$^{e}$ siècle, la machine nous a imposé une forme sans précédent d'organisation sociale, c'est-à-dire une économie de marché, qui s'est révélée être un simple épisode de l'histoire » (p. 522). Cette erreur de diagnostic n'enlève rien à la pertinence de ses analyses sur les méfaits du marché et à l'actualité de son plaidoyer en faveur d'une problématisation conjointe de l'économie et du politique. Ainsi les propos sur le dépassement de l'économie de marché vont de pair avec une réflexion sur la nature de la démocratie et la pluralité de ses formes (chap. 36). Relisant Aristote, Polanyi fait de la liberté la question centrale de « la vie bonne ». Préoccupé par la restriction des libertés par la machine et le conformisme, il insiste sur le fait que les libertés ne sont pas vouées à disparaître avec le marché. Bien au contraire, elles sont appelées à s'étendre hors de la sphère intellectuelle et politique vers la vie quotidienne et le monde du travail. Polanyi va jusqu'à formuler des propositions concrètes à cette fin (p. 564), considérant que la liberté humaine se mesure d'abord à la liberté de choisir.

Au-delà de la mise en évidence de la pluralité des formes économiques et de leur articulation avec le politique, ce livre adresse de front les problèmes moraux posés par le capitalisme et soulève la question des conditions d'une existence humaine libre et pleinement responsable. Dans une postface qui reprend un article déjà paru en 2007[1], Alain Caillé et Jean-Louis Laville soulignent l'actualité de la pensée de Polanyi en ce qu'elle apporte la démonstration magistrale que le marché n'est pas la matrice de la démocratie et de la liberté.

1. Dans le numéro de la *Revue du Mauss* titré « Avec Karl Polanyi, contre la société du tout marchand », 2007, n° 29.

# RECENSION D'OUVRAGE

*Économie de la justice et de l'équité*
Valérie Clément, Christine Le Clainche et Daniel Serra
Paris, Economica, 2008

GEERT DEMUIJNCK*

Les travaux de quelques économistes et philosophes, maintenant célèbres, des années 70 du siècle dernier ont donné le coup d'envoi à un développement assez spectaculaire d'un champ interdisciplinaire qui analyse les questions de justice sociale et de l'équité économique. Du côté philosophique, c'est avant tout l'œuvre de John Rawls [1971] qui a joué un rôle important. De l'autre côté, des économistes comme Amartya Sen [1970] ou Serge-Christophe Kolm [1972] ont développé la voie ouverte, entre autres, par Arrow [1951] d'un traitement formel des questions de justice sociale et de l'équité, qui, à son tour, ont stimulé le débat philosophique.

Un élément qui a certainement contribué au rapprochement des deux disciplines est que le fameux « principe de différence » de John Rawls, qui stipule qu'une inégalité sociale peut se justifier (si certaines autres conditions, que je laisse de côté ici, sont satisfaites) dans la mesure où ces inégalités sont au bénéfice du groupe le plus mal loti de la société, se prêtait presque de façon évidente à une reprise plus formelle par des économistes de l'économie normative

* EDHEC Business School, Lille.

et des théoriciens du choix social. L'économie normative est la branche de la théorie économique qui ambitionne de comparer les différents états sociaux (et indirectement les différents arrangements institutionnels et politiques publiques qui les déterminent) selon le critère du bien-être social, défini comme la somme du bien-être des individus. Le bien-être individuel (en anglais *welfare*, ce qui explique pourquoi on appelle cette branche *welfare economics*) est défini à son tour comme le degré de satisfaction des préférences. La théorie du choix social s'est développé à partir des limites qu'imposait ce cadre théorique welfariste, soulignées par Kenneth Arrow [1951]. Elle prouve et interprète des théorèmes (d'impossibilité, d'unicité de solution, etc.) qui concernent l'agrégation des préférences et des intérêts des individus, sur la base de différents axiomes représentant des caractéristiques souhaitables de l'agrégation.

L'ouvrage coécrit par Valérie Clément, Christine Le Clainche et Daniel Serra est avant tout une présentation structurée de ce développement spectaculaire du champ interdisciplinaire entre philosophie politique et théorie économique. Comme le titre l'indique, il se focalise sur ce développement du côté de la théorie économique et, plus largement, des sciences sociales. Il présente également les développements philosophiques, mais ici l'ouvrage présente surtout les débats philosophiques qui ont été pertinents pour les économistes. Certains développements, également développés par les disciples et critiques de Rawls, comme le débat sur justice internationale par exemple, ont logiquement été laissé de côté. Les auteurs ont également laissé de côté les multiples applications de ce développement théorique dans les travaux des économistes qui concernent les politiques de la santé, de l'éducation, du logement, etc.

L'ambition du livre est clairement annoncée : rendre accessible cette littérature contemporaine sur la justice et l'équité aux économistes d'abord, mais également à un public plus large. Par conséquent, la formalisation a été réduite au minimum. On pourrait penser que cette ambition est assez limitée, dans la mesure où les auteurs ne prétendent pas ajouter une pierre originale à cet édifice, mais se limitent à le présenter et à le rendre accessible. Mais, en réalité, il s'agit d'un réel défi, tellement le champ est large et exigeant dans la mesure où il demande une capacité de lecture et de synthèse étendue, allant des développements formels des théoriciens du choix social aux traités philosophiques. Les auteurs maitrisent un champ de littérature très large et la première utilité de ce livre est de mettre en perspective les différentes variantes de ce foisonnement de théories de la justice. La première partie du livre (chap. 1 et 2) retrace le rapprochement des champs théoriques en esquissant d'abord l'évolution de l'économie normative traditionnelle vers une théorie économie de la justice et en présentant le « labyrinthe » des théories modernes de la justice. Les deux chapitres suivants sont les plus formels de l'ouvrage. Le chapitre 3 développe la théorie du choix social et présente en détail la discussion autour du théorème d'agrégation de John Harsanyi et le chapitre 4 développe les théories économiques de l'équité. Ensuite viennent deux chapitres qui partent d'un débat philosophique pour présenter les travaux des économistes qui se situent dans le prolongement de ce débat. Le chapitre 5 présente ainsi les différentes conceptions de la notion d'impartialité développées par, d'une part, John Harsanyi, et, d'autre part John Rawls. Les critiques réciproques des deux conceptions mènent vers des développements théoriques proposés par Arneson, Roemer, Fleurbaey ou encore Sen. Le chapitre 6 présente le débat égalitariste contemporain et montre comment la discussion autour de la notion de responsabilité, introduite par Dworkin, a mené vers des travaux formels sur l'égalité des opportunités (Roemer, Van de Gaer). Une septième chapitre présente assez brièvement les courants philosophiques alternatifs, c'est-à-dire ni utilitaristes ni égalitaristes. Finalement, et c'est sans doute l'aspect le plus original du livre, les auteurs ont intégré les contributions théoriques des économistes (et des autres sciences sociales) en dehors de l'économie normative : ils présentent en deux chapitres les approches « positives » de la justice et de l'équité. L'un se concentre sur les comportements observés des individus qui s'expliquent en termes de justice ou d'équité. L'autre focalise sur les tests empiriques de justice. C'est dans ce dernier chapitre qu'on retrouve aussi une brève présentation des travaux empiriques des auteurs de l'ouvrage.

Un point important concernant ce champ interdisciplinaire est de ne pas se mélanger les pinceaux entre une argumentation *normative* sur ce qui est souhaitable et une approche *positive* qui étudie (décrit ou explique) les comportements. En principe, le débat sur la justice distributive est de nature normative et porte sur la façon dont les bénéfices et les charges devraient, idéalement, être distribué dans la société. Si ce travail normatif intéresse le monde réel, c'est en tant qu'instrument d'évaluation et comme source d'inspiration d'éventuelles réformes. Les sciences sociales, en revanche, sont caractérisées par une approche positive du comportement, des normes sociales et des institutions, qu'elles essayent de décrire ou d'expliquer en tant que faits. Des scientifiques sociaux peuvent juger des propositions de réforme sur leur faisabilité, mais non pas sur leur légitimité.

Par rapport à cette dichotomie, l'économie normative et la théorie du choix social occupent une position ambiguë. D'une part, ces théories sont normatives, mais dans un sens très limité : elles développent un cadre formel qui permet d'examiner des principes normatifs, non pas concernant leur désirabilité, mais concernant leur compatibilité logique avec d'autres principes (normatifs ou autres). Elles examinent la consistance logique des combinaisons des caractéristiques désirables des fonctionnelles de bien-être social (*social welfare functions*, c'est-à-dire, des classements des états sociaux) : « Ce travail relève de l'analyse logique (étude de la compatibilité mutuelle des axiomes) et/ou économique (étude de l'existence d'allocations, ou de la non-vacuité de règles d'allocations) » [Fleurbaey 1996, 4].

Autrement dit, la théorie du choix social est une discipline *mathématique* qui prouve des théorèmes basés sur des axiomes qui correspondent (ou sont supposés correspondre) aux principes moraux ou rationnels. La signification pleinement normative de ces travaux dépend non seulement de l'interprétation des théorèmes, mais aussi de la pertinence des principes moraux sous-jacents dans une justification éthique. Du point de vue méthodologique, si ces théories ne sont évidemment pas positives dans le sens où elles décriraient ou expliqueraient des faits, elles ne sont pas *éthiquement normatives* non plus. Aux balbutiements du développement de ce champ interdisciplinaire, il y a eu pas mal de confusion sur ces points. Ici, les auteurs ont pris soin de clarifier ces points dans l'introduction et à différents autres endroits, afin d'aider le lecteur à éviter ces pièges épistémologiques.

Dans la mesure où les auteurs ne défendent pas de position particulière dans le débat philosophique ni présentent des travaux positifs originaux, l'objet de ce compte rendu est limité. On pourrait éventuellement avancer des remarques sur le fait que tel auteur ou théorie a reçu trop ou pas assez d'attention dans cet ouvrage, mais ce ne serait pas équitable face à l'ampleur du projet. Toutefois, j'aurais une critique ou plutôt suggestion, dans le cas où le travail serait repris ultérieurement, concernant la façon dont li libertarisme a été traité. Les auteurs ont eu raison d'intégrer une présentation du libertarisme dans l'ouvrage. Les critiques de Rawls par Nozick ont en effet profondément influencé les développements post-rawlsiens, aussi bien ceux des philosophes que ceux des économistes. Cette présentation a été intégrée dans un chapitre intitulé « Des courants de pensée alternatifs : libertarisme et communautarisme ». Toutefois, contrairement au libertarisme, le courant communautarien n'a pas eu d'influence significative sur le développement du champ interdisciplinaire de la justice et de l'équité. Au contraire, Charles Taylor a qualifié l'impression de précision que suggère la formalisation du concept de justice de « bogus » [Taylor 1982, 143]. Une alternative pourrait être de laisser de côté le communautarisme et d'élargir ce chapitre sur la libéralisme vers un chapitre, à l'instar du précédent, sur la liberté, car aussi concernant cette notion la rencontre entre économistes et philosophes a été fructueuse (par exemple Laslier *et alii* [1997], mais aussi les travaux de Pattanaik et Xu, Puppe, Carter, Van Hees, etc.).

## RÉFÉRENCES

ARROW K., 1951, *Social choice and individual values*, New York, Wiley, 2e ed. 1963.

FLEURBAEY M., 1996, *Théories économiques de la justice*, Paris, Economica.

KOLM S.-Ch., 1972, *Justice et équité*, Paris, Éditions du CNRS.

LASLIER J.-F., FLEURBAEY M., GRAVEL N. et TRANNOY A. (eds.), 1997, *Freedom in Economics: New Perspectives in Normative Analysis*, Londres, Routletge.

SEN A., 1970, *Collective Choice and Social Welfare*, Amsterdam, North-Holland.

RAWLS J., 1971, *A Theory of Justice*, Oxford, Oxford UP.

TAYLOR Ch., 1982, « The diversity of goods », *in* A. Sen and B. Williams (eds.), *Utilitarianism and beyond*, Cambridge, Cambridge UP, p. 129-144.

# RECENSION D'OUVRAGE

*Institutions and the Path to the Modern Economy. Lessons from Medieval Trade*
Avner Greif
Cambridge, Cambridge UP, 2006

CYRIL HÉDOIN *

*Institutions and the Path to the Modern Economy* d'Avner Greif s'inscrit dans le prolongement d'une littérature que l'on a vu fortement se développer ces dernières décennies autour de l'économie des institutions. Néanmoins, cet ouvrage se veut être davantage qu'une simple contribution supplémentaire à ce champ : comme l'annonce explicitement l'auteur, ce travail se présente comme une tentative de dépassement des différentes traditions en sciences sociales et de leurs apories, à partir d'une nouvelle approche qu'il baptise « *institutional dynamics as an historical process* » [p. 155].

L'objectif de l'ouvrage est en effet ambitieux : en s'appuyant sur ses propres travaux s'étalant sur plus de 20 ans et portant sur les économies européennes et maghrébines du Moyen Âge, et en combinant différentes traditions théoriques (théorie des jeux, sociologie, sciences politiques), l'auteur se propose d'élaborer un cadre générique d'analyse des institutions tout en offrant un éclairage

* Université de Reims Champagne-Ardenne, UFR des sciences économiques, sociales et de gestion, 57 bis rue Pierre Taittinger 51096 Reims, cyril.hedoin@univ-reims.fr.

nouveau sur certains épisodes historiques concernant les économies du Moyen Âge. L'ouvrage défend deux thèses, l'une historique, l'autre théorique. Sur le plan historique, l'auteur entend montrer que, dans une large mesure, l'origine de l'économie de marché dans les pays développés se trouve dans le processus d'évolution des institutions partant des économies européennes du Moyen Âge. Sur le plan théorique, Greif cherche à établir que la théorie des jeux, combinée à des études de cas empiriques, peut constituer le socle d'une théorie à même de rendre compte du processus d'évolution endogène des institutions.

L'espace étant restreint, on ne tentera pas ici de faire un résumé de l'ouvrage. On se contentera de souligner certains des enjeux qui en ressortent et qui sont susceptibles d'initier une discussion. En effet, selon nous, les analyses et l'argumentation d'Avner Greif posent au moins autant de questions qu'elles n'apportent de réponses. Comme cela est très souvent le cas avec ce type de travaux d'envergure, ambitionnant la construction d'une nouvelle approche, le lecteur ressort à la fois stimulé par les innovations introduites mais aussi réservé, ou au moins dubitatif, sur un certain nombre de points. Pour cette note de lecture, on en relèvera deux qui suscitent à la fois l'intérêt et posent des questions.

Le premier élément de réflexion est l'utilisation que fait Greif de la théorie des jeux. Implicitement, tout au long de l'ouvrage, il apparaît que « théorie » et « théorie des jeux » sont utilisées de manière synonyme. L'auteur s'attache longuement à défendre, de façon plutôt convaincante, son usage de la théorie des jeux. A ce titre, au moins deux points méritent réflexion : en premier lieu, le rejet par l'auteur de la théorie des jeux évolutionnaire et d'autres formes de modélisations évolutionnaires au profit des jeux répétés ne peut qu'attirer l'attention de quiconque s'intéresse à la question des institutions en économie. En effet, la théorie des jeux évolutionnaire est, depuis près d'une trentaine d'années avec les travaux précurseurs de Robert Axelrod et William Hamilton [1981], un des outils privilégiés des économistes, y compris hétérodoxes et donc, *a priori*, moins enclins à la modélisation. Les critiques qu'adresse Greif à son encontre ne peuvent être ignorées : si la théorie des jeux (répétés) reposent sur des hypothèses non réalistes, il en va exactement de même concernant les modèles évolutionnaires (hypothèse de myopie des agents par exemple), qui de plus ne prennent en compte que les mécanismes d'apprentissage individuel. Cette argumentation appelle indéniablement à une réflexion sur la pertinence comparée des différentes modélisations évolutionnaires et celles des jeux répétés. D'autre part, l'introduction par Greif de nouveautés techniques telles que la notion de « quasi-paramètre » mérite d'être discutée : dans le cadre des jeux répétés, les paramètres sont des « règles du jeu » exogènes, fixées par le modélisateur et considérées comme invariables. L'introduction d'un quasi-paramètre consiste à supposer qu'au fur et à mesure que le jeu est répété, un des paramètres (par exemple, les gains issus de la coopération mutuelle des deux joueurs) va évoluer de manière endogène en $t$ en fonction du résultat en $t-1$. L'introduction du concept de quasi-paramètre permet ainsi de rendre compte des effets de l'institution étudiée sur l'environnement socio-économique : il parait sensé de supposer par exemple qu'une institution assurant la coopération entre deux clans est susceptible d'accroître la richesse globale d'une ville et, par conséquent, de rendre les gains issus de la coopération plus importants dans le futur. Cette technique permet également de rendre compte du fait qu'un changement dans l'environnement (les paramètres) ne conduit pas nécessairement à la disparition ou à la modification d'une institution (l'équilibre du jeu). Si cette innovation saisie incontestablement un mécanisme institutionnel significatif (l'impact d'une institution sur l'environnement socio-économique), elle renforce l'impression du caractère *ad hoc* qui est souvent reproché à la théorie des jeux.

Ce dernier élément mène directement au deuxième point de réflexion : celui de l'articulation entre théorie et histoire. Cette question est en effet le véritable fil rouge de l'ouvrage de Greif. Alors que la science économique a souvent été accusée d'ignorer l'histoire, la démarche de Greif ne peut que susciter l'attention. Il en ressort que le travail de ce dernier est, sans être un travail d'historien, un travail tenant compte et portant sur l'histoire. L'auteur mobilisent des connaissances historiques, assises sur plus de 20 ans de recherche, donnant à son travail une consistance historique qui est relativement peu fréquente en économie. Un point suscite néanmoins une interrogation. Bien que l'articulation entre l'histoire (les études de cas) et la théorie (la modélisation par la théorie des jeux) soit exposée de manière claire dans les parties méthodologiques de l'ouvrage, la relation apparaît moins évidente lorsque des cas spécifiques sont abordés. Ainsi, en dépit de sa critique développée au chapitre 10 à l'encontre du modèle de Milgrom, North et Weingast [1990], au motif qu'il pêcherait par son manque d'articulation avec le contexte historique, on peut avoir l'impression que l'auteur adopte une démarche rigoureusement identique : une sélection *a priori* du matériau historique qui débouche sur un modèle testant une seule conjecture. Incontestablement, le passage d'un matériau historique qualitatif infiniment complexe à une modélisation formelle forcément réductrice pose des difficultés épistémologiques, qui sont d'ailleurs plus évidentes lorsque l'auteur formule des conjectures historiques plus amples. Pour l'essentiel, les conjectures formulées dans l'ouvrage portent à chaque fois sur un épisode historique précis et bien identifié. En revanche, l'hypothèse plus générale formulée par l'auteur sur la filiation entre l'économie de marché et les institutions des économies européennes du Moyen Âge n'est pas elle-même « testée » par un modèle formel. Elle est élaborée à partir de l'association d'analyses empiriques isolées et choisies par l'auteur. En amont de l'analyse formelle, une sélection des épisodes historiques jugés pertinents est ainsi nécessairement opérée. De même, en aval, une interprétation des résultats théoriques obtenus est requise. Dans les deux cas, les procédés utilisés sont non formels (analyse de textes par exemple, ou encore spéculations sur le rôle de la religion dans la formation de clans, p. 389). Ces deux éléments réunis contribuent à donner un « sens à l'histoire » que la seule modélisation par la théorie des jeux ne peut permettre de formaliser. On peut ainsi déceler une tendance au « *storytelling* » [McCloskey 1998] consistant à décrire le passage d'un état donné (l'Europe médiévale) à un état nouveau (l'économie de marché moderne) à partir d'une mise en cohérence *a posteriori* des résultats issus de la théorie. D'une certaine manière, si on peut estimer que cette tendance est inhérente à tout travail scientifique (surtout lorsqu'il a une dimension historique), il reste que l'auteur ne la reconnaît pas explicitement. Enfin, on relèvera que Greif ne résout le problème de la spécificité historique [Hodgson 2001] que par un chemin détourné. La mise en avant répétitive par l'auteur de l'importance de construire des modèles tenant compte des spécificités du contexte étudié ne peut qu'être perçue de manière positive. Cependant, cette démarche part de la prémisse – qui peut être contestée – que le cadre de la théorie des jeux est pertinent pour rendre compte de *tout* épisode historique. On doit néanmoins souligner que l'auteur apporte des éléments méthodologiques convaincants et que cette démarche est cohérente avec la recherche d'une unité théorique qui est revendiquée au début de l'ouvrage.

Au final, l'importance épistémologique et analytique de l'ouvrage d'Avner Greif ne saurait être sous-estimée. La nature même du projet poursuivi, fonder une analyse institutionnelle unifiée embrassant diverses traditions en économie et en sociologie, attirera forcément l'attention de très nombreux chercheurs. Ce travail doit contribuer à asseoir un peu plus l'émergence de ce nouveau champ qu'est l'économie institutionnelle et peut, par la même occasion, offrir un terrain de rencontre privilégié pour les auteurs orthodoxes et hétérodoxes s'intéressant à la question des institutions.

## RÉFÉRENCES

AXELROD R. and HAMILTON W., 1981, « The Evolution of Cooperation », *Science*, 211 (4489), p. 1390-1396.

HODGSON G., 2001, *How Economics Forgot History. The Problem of Historical Specificity in the Social Sciences*, London, Routledge.

MCCLOSKEY D., 1998, *The Rhetoric of Economics*, London, The University of Wisconsin Press.

MILGROM P., NORTH D.C., WEINGAST B.R., 1990, "The Role of Institutions in the Revival of Trade: The Medieval Law Merchant, Private Judges, and the Champagne Fairs", *Economics and Politics*, 2(1), p. 1-23.

ACHEVÉ D'IMPRIMER
EN MARS 2010
PAR L'IMPRIMERIE
DE LA MANUTENTION
A MAYENNE
FRANCE
N° 10N-38

Dépôt légal : 1er trimestre 2010

## BULLETIN D'ABONNEMENT

*Revue de Philosophie Économique*

**Je soussigné(e), M./Mme**

Nom : ................................................ Prénom : ............................................
Institution : ....................................... N° TVA : ...........................................
Rue : ................................................... Numéro : ..........................................
C.P. : .............. Ville : ....................................... Pays : ................................

**commande :**

au prix de 50 euros TTC (frais de port inclus) pour la France et de 55 euros TTC (frais de port inclus) pour l'étranger

......... abonnement(s) annuel 2009 à la *Revue de Philosophie Économique* (deux numéros par an).

au prix de 30 euros TTC (frais de port en sus)

......... ex. du numéro 1, vol. 10, juillet 2009, *Enjeux éthiques en économie de la santé*, 978-2-7116-5200-6
......... ex. du numéro 2, vol. 9, décembre 2008, 978-2-7117-3511-2
......... ex. du numéro 1, vol. 9, juillet 2008, *Démocratie d'entreprise*, 978-2-7117-3510-5
......... ex. du numéro 14, 2006/2, 978-2-7117-3507-5
......... ex. du numéro 13, 2006/1, 978-2-7117-3506-8
......... ex. du numéro 9, 2004/1, *Le concept d'identité*, 978-2-7117-3502-0
......... ex. du numéro 8, 2003/2, 978-2-7117-3501-3
......... ex. du numéro 7, 2003/1, *Autour de John Rawls*, 978-2-7117-3500-6

**Paiement :**

- ❐ par chèque vancaire à l'ordre de « Librairie Philosophique J. Vrin » (joindre le chèque au bulletin d'abonnement)
- ❐ par règlement administratif (joindre le bon de commande au bulletin d'abonnement)

Date : ............................... Signature

**À renvoyer à :** Librairie Philosophique J. Vrin
À l'attention de Frédéric Mendès – fmendes@vrin.fr
6 place de la Sorbonne
75005 Paris – France